A Short History of Inequality

A Short History of Inequality

Michele Alacevich
and Anna Soci

agenda
publishing

To my parents, Eugenio and Dede

Michele Alacevich

To my daughter Valentina

Anna Soci

This edition first published in 2018 by Agenda Publishing

Agenda Publishing Limited
The Core
Science Central
Bath Lane
Newcastle upon Tyne
NE4 5TF

www.agendapub.com

ISBN 978-1-78821-048-5 (hardcover)
ISBN 978-1-78821-049-2 (paperback)

British Library Cataloguing-in-Publication Data
A catalogue record for this book is available from the British Library

Printed and bound in the UK by 4edge Ltd, Essex

Contents

Acknowledgments

The proposal by Brookings Institution Press that we write a book on the history of inequality afforded us a particularly propitious opportunity to organize and elaborate ideas that have been at the core of our work for some time, such as the surprising absence of the matter of inequality from the core of the economics discipline, the relationship between inequality and democracy, and the complex dynamics connecting within-country and between-country inequality with the phenomenon of globalization.

During these last few years, research centers on inequality have multiplied; databases have grown in scale, scope, and sophistication; and a burgeoning literature has developed. The debate today is much richer than it was only a few years ago. Writing this book at this time, thus, gave us the extraordinary opportunity to study and build on an astonishingly rich body of research.

If the disciplines that drove us to this subject are different – one author is an economist, the other one a historian – one place deserves special mention for the role it played in bringing our thoughts together: Columbia University.

The Italian Academy for Advanced Study in America at Columbia University has been home to both of us, providing perfect conditions for intensive work and exchange of ideas with the university's broader scholarly community. We are very grateful to the academy's director, David Freedberg, and fellows in the years 2009–10 and 2011–12 for the intellectual exchanges we were part of. Though we could not know it then, some roots of the present book date back to our work there.

The Heyman Center for the Humanities at Columbia University, in particular its director and chair, Mark Mazower, and its executive director, Eileen Gillooly, could not have been more supportive of the idea that economic inequality is a humanities subject par excellence. Indeed, the old boundaries between the humanities and the social sciences are no longer as delimited as they once were, and the Heyman Center is a powerhouse of new, cross-disciplinary thinking. Our work began while Anna Soci (the economist) was pursuing a research project on democracy and inequality at the Italian Academy and Michele Alacevich (the historian) was the associate director for research activities of the Heyman Center for the Humanities. Michele Alacevich is highly indebted to Mark Mazower, Eileen Gillooly, and the fellows in residence at the center throughout 2011–14 for the unique atmosphere of generous collaboration and intellectual curiosity.

We have given presentations on issues related to this book: at the International Colloquium on Inequality in Graz (2012), the European Economics and Finance Society Conference in Istanbul (2012) and Thessaloniki (2014), the Colloquium on Capitalism, Inequality and Democracy in Vancouver (2013), the Istituto Gramsci seminar on Inequality in Bologna (2013), the WINIR Conference in Greenwich (2014), and the Conference on Economic and Social Development in Vienna (2014). We are grateful for all the comments received from colleagues at those conferences, in particular Anna Maccagnan and Daniela Mantovani, who co-authored some of those papers with Anna Soci. Our students and colleagues in the "Rethinking Economics" network and the Collegio Superiore of the University of Bologna, Loyola University Maryland, Columbia University, and the Institute for New Economic Thinking (INET) in New York City have provided extremely valuable feedback on some of the issues discussed in this book.

Many friends and colleagues provided valuable comments on the entire manuscript or parts of it. In particular, we are indebted to Eugenio Alacevich, Mauro Boianovsky, Giorgio Colacchio, Giovanni De Lorenzo, Giovanna Dimitri, Mario Del Pero, Nando Fasce, Giorgio Gattei, Giovanni Giorgini, Ilene Grabel, Finola Hurley, Richard John, Nicola Melloni, Branko Milanovic, Enrico Petazzoni, Ruby Rheid Thompson, Roberto Scazzieri, Giorgio Tassinari, Stefano Toso, and Carl Wennerlind. A special thank you goes to Nadia Urbinati. Vanni Montani, librarian of the Department of Economics, provided fundamental research support.

We also want to thank the director of the Brookings Institution Press, Valentina Kalk, her colleagues William Finan and Janet Walker, copy editor Marjorie Pannell, and Brian Ostrander of Westchester Publishing Services for shepherding the book from initial conception to final production with high professionalism, good humour, and patience. We are also grateful to two anonymous reviewers for providing invaluable and detailed feedback on an earlier draft of this book. The Center for the Humanities of Loyola University Maryland generously provided financial support for the language revision and production of the book. Our sincere thanks go to the center's director, Mark Osteen, and its program coordinator, Patty Ingram.

Introduction

> All animals are equal. But some animals are more equal than others.
>
> George Orwell, *Animal Farm*

Inequality is one of the major political issues of our time; it is part and parcel of our lives. According to how we define it, inequality can also teach us how we think about the foundational values of our societies. Both the notion of inequality and the daily experience of it compel us to consider what is fair and unfair, and to continuously – though perhaps unconsciously – connect the political to the ethical.

Inequality embraces many different dimensions, as testified by current debates on social, political, economic, gender, educational, race, and health inequality. Moreover, and more significant, the importance of these dimensions has changed greatly, both historically and geographically; in many cases the very categories we use now would have sounded meaningless to people living in earlier times. Even today, many inequalities are still far from being universally recognized. An example is the apparently simple and self-evident issue of gender equality. Gender equality often is not accepted and, even when lip service is paid to the concept, not practiced. Though in different degrees, this applies not only to dictatorial countries where men enjoy a legal superiority over women but also in countries that consider themselves egalitarian (at least with respect to gender), such as Western democracies. Thus people may differ hugely in their opinions on inequality, not only in terms of what degree of inequality is considered acceptable or unacceptable but also, and more fundamentally, in terms of which inequalities are important since different people have different values at the core of their own moral universe. Because humans are social animals and inequality is, by definition, a relational dimension, discussions about equality and inequality are also discussions about a society's structure. For these reasons, constructing a short history of inequality is an impossible task – at least if one wants to do justice to such a complex and varied phenomenon.

One component of the broader inequality issue, however, both undergirds and takes its place alongside other inequalities: economic inequality.[1] Few would deny that economic inequality poses dramatic challenges to modern societies, both economically advanced and less developed ones. There is widespread agreement that inequality is a serious threat to the economic and political foundations of modern societies. According to former US Secretary of Labor Robert Reich, the United States is reaching, possibly has reached, the point at which inequality is so widespread as to imperil economic growth and democracy.[2] The Nobel laureate Joseph Stiglitz has remarked, "We pay a high price for this inequality, in terms of our democracy and nature of our society ... Our democracy is undermined, as economic inequality inevitably translates into political inequality."[3] This point is effectively summed up in an (apocryphal) observation by Supreme Court Justice Louis Brandeis (1856–1941): "We can have a democratic society or we can have the concentration of great wealth in the hands of a few. We cannot have both."[4] It bears emphasizing that these concerns are not exclusive to those on the left of the political spectrum (both Reich and Stiglitz were influential officers in the Clinton administration, and Brandeis was an antimonopolist progressive). Even strong believers in the virtues of a market economy, such as former Chairman of the Federal Reserve Alan Greenspan, a staunch market fundamentalist, admit as much. In a September 2007 interview he argued that "if you have the increasing sense that the rewards of capitalism are being distributed unjustly, the system will not stand."[5]

It is also widely agreed that inequality is not solely the domestic problem of affluent societies gone off-track. The world as a whole faces an inequality problem. The increasing international economic integration known as globalization – especially in its more recent phase, characterized by financial deregulation and the weakening of state sovereignty – has had an important effect on inequality dynamics, both domestically and globally. Three economists of the International Monetary Fund – a traditionally neoliberal, pro-globalization-as-we-know-it organization – recently wrote that the liberalization of international capital flows and the implementation of domestic austerity policies have not delivered as expected. In particular, economic inequality has increased – or remained stagnant at best – in most countries. As they argue, "Even if growth is the sole or main purpose of the neoliberal agenda, advocates of that agenda still need to pay attention to the distributional effects."[6]

Obviously, the overall picture is much more complex than these few comments suggest. For example, there is evidence that in the first decade of the twenty-first century inequality decreased in many populous Latin American countries, such as Argentina,

Brazil, and Mexico. Moreover, the growth of China and India and their catching up with the rich economies has greatly mitigated, at the global level, the sharply rising inequality observed in many countries between 1980 and 2000. And yet, despite their recent positive record, Latin American countries remain among the most unequal in the world. Likewise, global inequality, although apparently lower than in the early 2000s, is still much higher than in any single country, and also much higher than it was at the beginning of the twentieth century, or in the 1970s.[7]

In sum, despite a number of important caveats and qualifications with regard to specific countries and inequality indicators, the problem of widespread economic inequality is a major characteristic of the current global predicament and is central to current political and economic discourse both nationally and internationally. Thus, while remaining fully aware that we are discussing only one aspect – though an extremely relevant one – of a much broader picture, we will focus in these pages on that specific issue only.

Whereas economic inequality per se cannot be said to be a new issue, its catalytic power in terms of political discourse is indeed novel. How has a subject that, until recently, captured the attention of only a small group of economists become one of the most debated issues of the day? Our answer lies in a very simple – and certainly somber – observation. While we have been used to consider inequality as a basic characteristic of many less developed countries (except perhaps the very poor countries, whose low inequality is mainly attributable to everybody being poor), only in recent years have pundits, the economics profession at large, and public opinion awakened to the fact that inequality has become a fundamental and structural problem in countries that have long considered themselves immune from it – mainly the advanced countries. Inequality, in other words, has penetrated the developed world, whereas earlier it appeared to be mainly a problem of distant regions.

We could not explain otherwise the "Piketty phenomenon" – how Thomas Piketty's *Capital in the Twenty-First Century* turned into a publishing sensation when it was translated into English in 2014 – or the smaller but still remarkable success of other books, such as Richard Wilkinson and Kate Pickett's *The Spirit Level* (2009) and, more recently, Robert J. Gordon's *The Rise and Fall of American Growth* (2016), which, as its subtitle reveals, discusses the US standard of living since the Civil War and its disappointing record since the 1970s.[8] The financial crash of 2008 and its aftermath have also fueled a mounting debate in core capitalistic countries by dramatizing the question of the sustainability of radical inequality. As James K. Galbraith wrote in the opening sentence of his *Inequality and Instability*, "In the late 1990s, standard measures of income inequality in the United States … rose to levels not seen since 1929," the year of the Wall Street crash and the beginning of the Great Depression.[9]

In addition, the combination of surging inequality with what has been dubbed the third wave of globalization, or "hyperglobalization" (mid-1970s to the present), has provided a novel spin to inequality dynamics. In particular, the combination of inequality and globalization has affected social groups in different countries in diverse, and often mutually opposing, ways. For instance, the phenomenon of globalization has had a very different impact on the middle class of developed and less developed countries, helping some groups to better their position in the global income distribution while forcing other groups into stagnation.

Two categories are thus involved when we discuss inequality: an international and a domestic category. They have dynamics of their own, but are also interdependent. Inequality trends *between* countries combine with trends *within* countries to produce a broad spectrum of interrelated phenomena. Some of these are particularly visible at the national level, such as the crisis of middle-class incomes in advanced economies, the widening gap between the top 1 per cent and the rest, and the disruption of check and balances between economic and political power. Some of them, on the contrary, are intrinsically transnational, such as growing international migrations from poor to rich countries. These categories – the domestic and the international – are evidently related, and global causes surely have domestic effects in multiple countries more or less at the same time. Thus the *within*-country and *between*-country inequality concepts we will be calling on in this book are intended only as analytical tools to understand an underlying more unified system.

To continue with our examples, the crisis of the middle class in advanced economies has its counterpoint in the rise of a "middle class" in a number of emerging countries (the quote marks are necessary here, as this emerging middle class is still very poor when compared with the income levels of the middle class in older industrialized countries). International migrations affect the supply of labour and the ratio between skilled and unskilled labour both in countries of origin and in countries of destination. Globalization challenges state sovereignty and the efficacy of mechanisms of political representation. The related emergence of national populisms goes hand in hand with increasingly globalized oligarchic networks. The political dimension of inequality, and the political neglect of this question (until very recently), have historically undergirded these dynamics.

The observation of these interrelated processes is at the base of what in 2011 the Harvard political economist Dani Rodrik dubbed the "globalization paradox." Rodrik highlighted the political trilemma rooted in the unavoidable tension among (1) national sovereignty, (2) well-functioning democratic institutions, and (3) full-fledged economic globalization. In his analysis, largely shared by scholars and commentators, it is possible to have two elements together, but not three at the same time; one must be sacrificed.[10]

One barely need notice how major political events of the last few years exemplify different political responses to this unsustainable tension. The continuing euro crisis is testament to the conflict of sovereignty and democratic representation between national-level and European Union-level government in the face of increasing economic integration that, however, does not take the form of a proper transfer union. Unable to solve Rodrik's trilemma, the EU suffers from a deep democratic deficit. National sovereignty is weakened, and countries' ability to foster occupational, social, and equalizing policies is severely limited, thereby unleashing inequality forces. The 2015 Greek crisis was the quintessential demonstration of this malaise, with the so-called troika institutions (the European Commission, the European Central Bank, and the International Monetary Fund) dictating political and economic policies to the Greek government, de facto depriving the country's government of its sovereignty and the Greek people of their political agency.[11]

The withdrawal of Great Britain from the EU is a different response to the same conundrum, sacrificing in this case open borders to national sovereignty (although the Irish, Scottish, and Welsh people and their representative institutions, solidly against Brexit, have much to object to about the functioning of democratic representation within the borders of the United Kingdom). The first acts of the Trump administration – especially the withdrawal of the United States from the Trans-Pacific Partnership (a free-trade partnership), the support given to infrastructural national works (mainly to the benefit of the oil industry), the informal but very clear message that major productive activities such as the automobile industry must not delocalize, and the order to construct an anti-immigrant wall at the border with Mexico – are also a reaction, at least rhetorical, to the economic crisis of US middle-class and blue-collar workers, who feel overwhelmed and left behind by disruptive global forces such as international migrations and industrial delocalization. Whether an administration headed by an opaque construction magnate and populated with seasoned Wall Street people will actually be able to provide political representation for the blue-collar workers who voted for it is another question.

Very simply, globalizing processes feed inequality internationally and affect it domestically, and growing domestic inequality in turn affects global processes.

* * *

From the broad spectrum of problems related to inequality, global imbalances and the challenge to democracy are the two aspects we will discuss here, as examples of between-country and within-country inequality. Strongly interrelated as they are, they frame our age. We will take up these two aspects after first placing inequality in the context of the history of the economic discipline, looking for the reasons that impeded its full embedding in the discipline's epistemological statute.

Chapter 1 of this book presents a synthesis of opposing positions on the inequality debate, and some elements useful in navigating the question of why inequality matters (if it matters at all). Despite the current centrality of the inequality debate in public discourse, some scholars and pundits consider the focus on inequality misleading and unimportant. By now it will be evident that we believe inequality to be a crucial issue of the contemporary world, but it is important to map out opposing views as well. To be clear, nobody in this debate is in favor of inequality per se, although some consider a certain degree of inequality beneficial, for it fosters saving, capital accumulation, and ultimately growth. The debate instead revolves around a different question, that is, whether we should focus on inequality or on other issues, such as poverty, or the ability to conduct a dignified life, or economic growth.

The historical analysis starts properly with chapter 2 and continues in chapter 3. In these chapters we discuss how the economic thought on inequality has developed in the last three centuries or so. In particular, we discuss a question that we deem important both for the history of economic inequality studies and for our understanding of current debates, namely, why inequality has for a very long time remained on the margins of economic discourse. The economy is often the principal focus of political discussion today, and economists have become the quintessential experts on how to fix social problems, yet until very recently economic inequality was consistently and stubbornly ignored. Turning inequality into a subject of statistical analysis, we argue, has been an elegant way to veil its true nature and marginalize it.

Chapters 4 and 5 address two contemporary issues, the relationship between globalization and inequality and that between inequality and democracy. Both issues powerfully shape the world in which we live and are particularly important for current political debates. As a consequence, we give them special weight in our analysis, considering each of them as valuable examples of, respectively, the between- and within-country dimensions of inequality.

Finally, chapter 6 addresses policy debates, offering a bridge to the (near) future. In other words, what discussions are shaping the current debate in a lasting fashion? What are the questions that seem to be relevant for the future of inequality? We are well aware that we walk here on particularly thin ice. And yet it is important, if only as an analytical exercise, to try to imagine how the current debate may evolve.

Unfortunately, economic inequality is a technical and complicated subject when discussed by insiders, and, like other branches of economics, it is highly mathematized. We have avoided these technicalities as much as possible, turning the inescapable ones into plain words. The appendix at the end of the book offers a brief discussion of the main concepts, databases, and calculations, to show the tools that underwrite our discussions and the meticulous work that economists do to refine concepts and information and offer increasingly reliable and plausible data to the community of scholars, government officials, and the public.

This seems a tall order for a short book, and indeed it is. But short books have at least one positive characteristic (besides being short): they force authors to stick to the essential matter and prompt them to be highly selective. Obviously, we have relied heavily on the cutting-edge research that many leading scholars are producing on subjects we can discuss only cursorily here. This book is certainly not alternative to the fundamental studies by Anthony B. Atkinson, François Bourguignon, Angus Deaton, James K. Galbraith, Branko Milanovic, Thomas Piketty, and Joseph E. Stiglitz, to name only a few of the most renowned scholars of development and inequality.

Still, this book has a precise distinctiveness. Besides introducing the lay reader to the main concepts and debates of inequality studies, it discusses how inequality has long been marginalized in the economics field and how inequality is shaping two fundamental issues of our epoch: globalization and democracy. Whether we succeed in giving globalization a human face and keeping democracy a credible and truly representative political system will depend in greatest part on how we resolve the problem of inequality.

ONE

Why Inequality Is the Real Issue

> For unto every one that hath shall be given, and he shall have abundance: but from him that hath not shall be taken away even that which he hath.
>
> Matthew 25:29

Inequality is not new. In fact, it has accompanied civilization at least since human societies discovered sedentary agriculture, between 11,000 and 8,000 years ago. Anthropological research has shown the markedly egalitarian basis of social and economic relations in hunter-gatherer societies, but the loss of nomadic habits and the increasingly sedentary character of human groups after the invention of agriculture meant the growth and evolution of much more complex economies and social structures – hence social stratification, clientage networks, and the emergence of ruling elites that were able to use violence freely to their own ends.[1] As the Nobel laureate Angus Deaton recently wrote, "Inequality is one of the 'gifts' of civilization."[2]

What is new is rather the centrality of inequality to the

contemporary public debate. As this book argues, the matter of inequality comes into starker view with increasing globalization (though in complicated ways) and contributes in crucial ways to the fissure in the social compact and the collapse of political processes in many modern societies, both economically developed and less developed.

In the post-Second World War period, key socioeconomic perspectives were visible in such common expressions as "the war on poverty" and "the welfare state." The recent spate of crises – economic, social, political, crises of representation and sovereignty – calls into question the adequacy of those perspectives to explain the contemporary era. It is not by accident that inequality has emerged with increasing force as a key dimension, for it is one of the engines driving these crises.

INEQUALITY AS A NONPROBLEM?

Many politicians, pundits, and scholars argue that the inequality issue should be expunged outright from the political and scholarly agenda. In some cases, this position has been adopted for clearly opportunistic reasons. The 2012 Republican presidential candidate, billionaire Mitt Romney, for example, considered claims of inequality to be "very envy oriented" and hence to be kept out of public debate.[3] More generally, many have shared the fear that doing something about inequality might endanger the status quo. Even scholars of good repute have exhibited a rather nonchalant attitude, suggesting that a certain degree of inequality must be accepted to maintain a society in good political and economic health: William Nozick is a notable example, and in the early nineteenth century Alexis de Tocqueville argued very much the same.

Others, finally, claim that not inequality but poverty is the real problem, and that global diffusion of economic growth is the answer. Deirdre McCloskey, for example, has recently made the case that inequality is a false problem and that "the absolute condition of the poor has been raised overwhelmingly more by the Great Enrichment than by ... redistribution" – the Great Enrichment being McCloskey's term for the Industrial Revolution and its consequences for the well-being of people living in the countries that experienced it.[4] A graph of the average per capita income from the age of hunter-gatherers to present times, McCloskey argues, would resemble an ice-hockey stick, horizontal for tens of thousands of years, then abruptly surging after 1800 with the spread of the Industrial Revolution and economic growth. Inequality, in this scenario, is, for McCloskey, a nonissue: "The share of the bottom 10 per cent is irrelevant to the noble and ethically relevant and actually attainable purpose of raising the poor to a condition of dignity."[5]

In a similar vein, the Columbia University economist Jagdish Bhagwati has described inequality studies as "ludicrous," "irrelevant data mongering," and finally "a lunacy."[6] The philosopher Harry Frankfurt once characterized the moral importance of economic equality as "drily formalistic," "fetishistic," and "alienating." He added, however, that even though economic equality is not of moral importance, there are often good practical reasons for governments to be concerned with problems of economic distribution, as egalitarian social policies are important to fulfill fundamental needs such as nutrition and access to basic health.[7]

The list of arguments against inequality-as-a-problem could easily be extended. There is no need to proceed with a point-by-point analysis of all of those arguments. More interesting is to notice how they happen to fit the typical rhetorical tools of reactionary thought. One of them is the idea that economic inequality, far from being the unfortunate downside of an imperfect social and economic structure, actually fosters growth. *Curbing inequality, thus, would kill growth.* Albert O. Hirschman has called this the "jeopardy thesis," for according to this view, the cost of reducing inequality would endanger a much more precious accomplishment, in this case economic growth, which eventually benefits both rich and poor – or, as the saying goes, lifts all boats. Historical evidence, however, shows a different story: the thirty glorious years of postwar sustained economic growth corresponded to lower levels of inequality, at least in advanced economies. The growth-anemic recent decades, on the contrary, have instead witnessed a dramatic increase in inequality.[8]

Second, there is the thesis according to which fighting inequality distorts certain inner mechanisms of modern societies that are based in the free unfolding of individual talents and preferences, which makes social mobility possible. *Curbing inequality, thus, would become an obstacle to improving one's own position* (except perhaps for social "parasites"). This is a version of what Hirschman calls the "perversity thesis," according to which any action to improve the social and economic order ends up worsening the initial situation. In fact, there is solid evidence that in recent decades, inequality has increased even as social mobility has almost completely stopped.

Third, we encounter the idea that *inequality does not matter, and even if it did matter, nothing can be done about it.* This is a perfect example of what Hirschman has called the "futility thesis," that is, the idea that every effort to redress the current state of things is doomed, and hence there is no point in trying. Another version of this thesis is that *other issues, such as poverty and education, are important for society, but not inequality.* This version of the futility thesis reflects the idea that a society consists of unrelated segments that are mutually independent. This construct is patently untrue. And though structural inequality is not easy to address, history provides many examples of policies that were successful in curbing inequality.[9]

INEQUALITY AND POVERTY

Before the worldwide recession of 2008–9, research agendas related to both developed and less developed countries showed a strong preference for focusing on poverty and ignoring inequality as a problem. This one-sided predilection was probably the result of the different political implications embedded in the two concepts. While poverty may be smoothed as a nonantagonistic question, inequality will always, sooner or later, trigger a discussion about the structure of power and social disparities in a given society. As Branko Milanovic recalls in *The Haves and the Have-Nots*, the head of a prestigious US think tank once told him that "the think-tank's board was very unlikely to fund any work that had *income* or *wealth inequality* in its title," whereas a project with *poverty* in its title would have been perfectly fine.[10]

Similarly, the World Bank, the leading global aid organization in the postwar period, has been remarkably indifferent to the problem of inequality, and not for a lack of awareness.[11] Notably, the problem of inequality was recognized by the World Bank more than forty years ago. When the fifth president of the World Bank, Robert S. McNamara (1968–81), reorganized the bank's agenda, he made explicit reference to this issue. As he argued in a 1973 speech, "If we look objectively at the world today, we must agree that it is characterized by a massive degree of inequality. The difference in living standards between the rich nations and the poor nations is a gap of gigantic proportions ... Further, we must recognize that a high degree of inequality exists not only between developed and developing nations but within the developing nations themselves."[12] And yet, when it came to policy proposals, inequality as a target all but disappeared, its place taken by antipoverty policies, which were politically more palatable. Obviously, though not necessarily, poverty and inequality are often related. Reorienting development strategies toward rural areas where the bulk of the poor live was one way to address absolute poverty, but it also served to redress excessively skewed distributions of income.

The factual correlation between poverty and inequality, however, does not mean that the two are one and the same. Reducing poverty is often a good strategy to reduce inequality, and sometimes poverty is indeed a priority. Still, the two concepts are different and may be open to different and sometimes opposed dynamics. Economic growth may occur and poverty may decrease even as inequality increases. The economic history of the United States since the 1980s demonstrates these co-occurring trends.

INEQUALITY AND EQUALITY

The matter of inequality, in sum, has emerged only discontinuously in the social sciences. Until recently, inequality was a small and rarely studied subject, suppressed by either sovereign indifference or by a philosophically more compelling discussion of its "ideal" counterpart, equality.

To illustrate the disinterest that has long characterized academic attention to inequality, it suffices to observe how inequality has been removed from the landscape of social inquiry. All major dictionaries of social sciences, for example, discuss the philosophical foundations of equality at length. One can browse through the pages of the *Oxford Dictionary of the Social Sciences*, the *Encyclopedia of the Social Sciences*, the *Dictionary of the History of Ideas*, or the *Stanford Encyclopedia of Philosophy* and routinely find entries on equality. Inequality, on the contrary, only rarely has an entry of its own, and it is often limited to a specific dimension of the term. The highly authoritative *Encyclopaedia Britannica*, for example, has an entry on inequality – yet only as a mathematical concept. As a first attempt to remedy this lacuna, a contribution on inequality appeared in the 2014 Yearly Review of the *Britannica*, but it was limited to a discussion of economic inequality in the United States. A partial exception is the *New Palgrave Dictionary of Economics*, which, being devoted to a specific field, has a few entries on economic inequality, specifically with regard to material welfare, gender-related income inequality, and international inequality.

On the contrary, inequality and equality could be considered two sides of the same coin. The philosopher and Nobel laureate in economics Amartya Sen has been particularly effective in linking the two subjects, and, after he contributed some of the most important analyses of inequality in the economics literature, his work has become a standard reference in discussions of the moral philosophy and political economy of equality.

Sen argues that the question of equality is at the core of all major schools of thought concerned with the social life of human beings. "A common characteristic of virtually all the approaches to the ethics of social arrangements that have stood the test of time," he writes in *Inequality Reexamined*, "is to want equality of *something* – something that has an important place in the particular theory."[13] This "something" may be income, or levels of welfare, or utilities, or rights and liberties – different philosophical approaches have different priorities. But the central point, Sen claims, is that in some essential way, these different approaches are all "egalitarians."[14] Different schools of thought, in other words, part ways not so much in the importance they attach to equality per se but in what they consider the fundamental social dimension in which equality must be attained.

According to the focus of a specific philosophical approach, other dimensions will inevitably become less important and, if necessary, will be sacrificed to preserve the dimension of equality that is considered predominant. A libertarian, for example, will consider central that certain liberties are shared equally by all the individuals in a population. This, of course, does not hinder the libertarian from being content also with equality of incomes, but only to the point that it does not conflict with equality of liberties. Another position is the one inspired by John Rawls's *Theory of Justice*, according to which the prospects of the worse-off must always prevail, to the point of tolerating an unequal distribution if this improves the conditions of the poor.[15]

Sen thus concludes that the central question for discussions about equality is "equality of *what*?"[16] This question will necessarily receive different answers, depending on the diversity among individuals with respect to personal characteristics such as gender, age, and specific abilities, and the external circumstances that affect their lives, such as their wealth and the social environment in which they have been raised. In fact, it is impossible to discuss social interaction without considering the empirical fact of a deep and pervasive diversity of individuals. The idea of equity presupposes an actual diversity of initial conditions among individuals and groups, which implies, as a consequence, the need to level the playing field. Sen's "equality of what?" thus emerges as a forceful and pragmatic question with which to elucidate the idea of justice prevailing in a specific society.[17] Based on these reflections, Sen – and many scholars with him, most prominently Martha Nussbaum and Frances Stewart – have been working on a new theory of justice, one based on the concepts of the capabilities and functioning of individuals.[18]

INEQUALITY, BIG TIME

Whereas the ideal of equality has captured the attention of philosophers, the reality of inequality has also become inescapable. The recent collapse of the global economy had much to do with the fundamental structural role played by the remarkable and widespread growth of inequality, which has been on the rise in many important countries all along the development spectrum since the 1970s. This rise is an important and striking novelty, at least when compared with the experience of the generations that grew up in the three decades after the Second World War. We need only consider the increasingly skewed ratio of the average CEO's annual compensation to that of the typical worker, a metric that is often used to give an impressionistic idea of why today inequality is considered an urgent problem, whereas a few decades ago it was not. According to the Economic Policy Institute of Washington, DC, in 1965 CEO compensation in the United States was twenty-four times greater than that of the typical worker; in 1978 the ratio was 35 to 1; in 2007 it was 277 to 1; and in 2010, two years after the beginning of the global recession, it was 243 to 1.[19] According to Raghuram Rajan, former chief economist of the International Monetary Fund (IMF), even more worrisome is that the increasing divergence has taken place not only between billionaires (who belong to the top 1 per cent of the 1 per cent or higher of income distribution) and the rest of the population but also between those in the 90th wage percentile (that is, those whose wages are higher than the wages of 90 per cent of the rest of the wage-earning population) – say, office managers – and both those at the bottom of the wage ladder and those belonging to the middle class, whose earnings have remained virtually stagnant from the 1980s. In other words, according to Rajan, the major concern arises from the income stagnation of middle-class and blue-collar workers. This "fault line" or hidden fracture, as Rajan calls it, played a fundamental role in the earthquake that in 2008 shocked the financial sector and then propagated to the real economy.[20]

Nor was this the first time. As many commentators have noticed, the level of inequality in the United States before the crash of 2008 was unparalleled since the eve of the 1929 crash. The IMF economists Michael Kumhof and Romain Rancière, for example, noticed how both the crash of 1929 and that of 2008 were preceded by a sharp increase in income and wealth inequality, as well as an increase in the debt-to-income ratio of low- and middle-income families. James K. Galbraith noticed the same in the opening pages of his book *Inequality and Instability*.[21] The financial resources that were increasingly concentrated in the hands of the rich and the super-rich were diverted from consumption and sound investment opportunities to luxury consumption and – since "there is a limit to the number of Dom Pérignons and Armani suits one can drink or wear," as Milanovic joked – to financial speculation, thus fueling risky and eventually explosive bubbles.[22]

This increasing riskiness coincided with the frustration of the lower and middle classes, whose real income had long stagnated, and with the eagerness of the political class to maintain complacency among them – or, as Rajan writes, to "mollify" them – by easing access to credit.[23] As a result, consumption inequality increased much less than income inequality, creating a situation that, at least on the surface, appeared to work smoothly. This was the political side of the coin of increasing inequality between the rich and poorer segments of US society. "The interests of several large groups of people," Milanovic argued, "became closely aligned. High-net-worth individuals and the financial sector were ... keen to find new lending opportunities. Politicians were eager to 'solve' the irritable problem of middle-class income stagnation. The middle class and those poorer than them were happy to see their tight budget constraints removed as if by a magic wand."[24] And yet this implicit political bargain was at the same time generating increasing financial fragility. High-income households were able to recycle part of their growing incomes as loans to the rest of the population, which in turn could improve their consumption levels. In the absence of growth for poor and middle-class incomes, however, the structural result was increasing debt and leverage, and finally a major crisis.[25]

The stagnation of the real incomes of the lower classes is the other side of the coin of current high inequality, and many scholars have put forth explanations for this phenomenon. A thesis shared by a majority of scholars highlights the so-called skill-biased technological change that occurred in the last decades. According to this thesis, since production technologies in advanced countries are increasingly skilled-labour intensive, the relative incomes of unskilled workers have stagnated or fallen behind. Many thus argue that a major culprit of this increasing income inequality is the crisis in middle school and high school education that has characterized a number of industrial countries, most of all the United States.[26] The weaker strata of society have been unable to develop their educational, welfare, and social aptitudes and so have lagged increasingly behind.[27] According to this line of reasoning, the solution lies in accelerating the creation of new skills and processes of retraining.

Other scholars have questioned this "Transatlantic Consensus" on the skill-bias hypothesis. According to Anthony B.

Atkinson and James K. Galbraith, for instance, far from increasing, educational differentials have narrowed, de facto eroding the skill-bias hypothesis. What got wider instead were wage differentials as a result of a structural decline in the manufacturing sector, the momentous rise of low-paid service jobs, and, as others have also noticed, a process of politically induced decreasing unionization and (again politically induced) a decrease in top income tax rates, paired with a manifold increase in top income earnings. These analyses thus call for a political response significantly different from that prompted by the skill-bias hypothesis, one more strongly focused on macroeconomic industrial, labour, and fiscal policies.[28]

THE MULTIPRONGED NATURE OF INEQUALITY

Not only does structural inequality undermine the functioning of global and national economic systems, its disruptive power in the economic sphere also merges with other dimensions of inequality in a society, such as racial and gender inequality; inequality in education, opportunities, and other social attributes such as class and status; inequality in life expectancy; and, in less lucky countries, inequality in access to much more basic necessities, such as food and potable water. These inequalities reinforce each other (though not always in a linear way) to produce vicious circles, through a process called "cumulative causation," that entrap the most disadvantaged individuals or groups and make them lag increasingly behind the privileged ones.

Social scientists have often insisted on "self-reinforcing mechanisms," "critical thresholds," "dysfunctional institutions" and other forces that perpetuate existing stratifications and work against social mobility. Sociologists have highlighted the importance of "cultural capital" to explain how belonging to specific networks multiplies the opportunities of some to succeed in comparison with those who are excluded. Richard Sennett mentions Robert Merton's corollary to the so-called Peter principle: the higher one climbs up the social ladder, the less statistically probable it becomes that one falls down. Sennett himself has shown how self-respect can become increasingly easier to attain and maintain at higher levels of the social ladder than at lower ones.

Thus, inequality deeply penetrates the social fabric, shapes it, and remains engrained in it, possibly for generations. Inequality, in other words, is inherited.[29]

The forces of inequality operate also at the global level, and inequality is a crucial issue to explain the causes, effects, and implications of the current phenomenon of globalization. As a report by the International Labour Office (ILO) suggests, "New technology, supported by more open policies, has created a world more interconnected than ever before. This spans not only growing interdependence in economic relations – trade, investment, finance and the organization of production globally – but also social and political interaction among organizations and individuals across the world."[30] Globalization, in other words, directly affects the economic, political, and social life of individuals and groups within specific countries, as well as the economic and, consequently, power relations between different countries. These two kinds of inequality, usually referred to as "within-country" and "between-country" inequality, have somewhat different dynamics and histories but together contribute to global trends in inequality.

Perhaps one of the more visible and dramatic effects of the complex interaction of inequality dynamics within and between countries is the staggering volume of current global migrations. As Branko Milanovic notes, whereas in the early nineteenth century only 30 per cent of global inequality depended on average income differences among countries and 70 per cent depended on whether one was born rich or poor in one's own country, by the early twenty-first century the proportion was more than reversed: 80 per cent of global inequality today depends on the country where one is born, that is, on between-country inequality. If we add that current global communications make knowledge about the differences in income among nations much more accessible than before, it is not difficult to understand the powerful motivations behind millions of people who annually risk their lives to move to richer countries.[31] We discuss this subject further in chapter 4.

Last, and no less worrisome, inequality is a threat to the good functioning of democracies. This threat can hardly be exaggerated, as even opponents of egalitarianism covertly recognize. Economically unequal societies are more prone to political polarization, institutional malfunctioning, monopolistic practices, corruption, and government by the rich instead of by the people. Democracies affected by deep and increasing inequality, in sum, are at greater risk of a turn toward plutocracy and even kleptocracy. One of the main arguments of this book is that inequality imperils the mechanisms of a healthy democracy, as we discuss in chapter 5.[32]

First, however, we discuss the history of studies on economic inequality, as some knowledge of the long marginalization of this subject from the economics discipline is vital to understanding the current dramatic difficulty in tackling and managing it.

TWO

The Long Neglect of Inequality

> Equality is ... at once the most natural and the most chimerical of things.
>
> Voltaire, *Dictionnaire Philosophique*

In the second half of the eighteenth century, when Monsieur François-Marie Arouet, better known as Voltaire, wrote the sentence that appears as the epigraph to this chapter, inequality was a pressing problem, engrained in the social fabric. "It is impossible on our wretched globe," Voltaire wrote, "for men living in society not to be divided into two classes, one the rich who command, the other the poor who serve."[1] Those two classes comprised in turn a thousand different levels, which exhibited even more subtle differences. Inequality, Voltaire was saying, is intrinsic to human society and is the product of the innumerable differences that exist among individuals. Voltaire imagined a cook, the servant of a cardinal, daydreaming: "I am a man like my master, and I was born in tears, as he was. He will die with the same fear and the same rituals as I. Both of us perform the same natural functions. If the Turks conquered Rome, and I became cardinal and my master became the cook, I would take him into my service." Deep in his heart, the cook felt himself equal to his master. Inequality, Voltaire claimed, is a social reality, not an inherent part of human beings.

Voltaire's critique addressed a question that has characterized human societies at least since humans began aggregating in settled communities, sometime between 8000 and 6000 BCE, and he addressed it with an awareness that sprang from centuries-long discussions of poverty, status, and inequality.[2] Like his predecessors, and despite his deeply secular perspective, Voltaire too seemed to conclude that inequality was ineradicable. Most important, however, Voltaire considered inequality a mere consequence of another, deeper question: poverty. "All men would be necessarily equal," he wrote, "if they were without needs." He concluded, "It is the poverty characteristic of our species that subordinates one man to the other. The real evil is not inequality, but dependence."

Much to the satisfaction of the cardinal's cook, the world did turn upside down in 1789, although not at the hand of the Grand Turk, and *égalité* became one of the leading ideals of the French Revolution. Yet those hopes were short-lived, and reaction ensued. The inequality question never percolated into that mix of moral philosophy and economic analysis that came to be known as classical political economy, even when we consider authors sympathetic to the message of the Enlightenment and the revolution. In a similar vein, the poverty issue was also virtually buried after a brief appearance. The realization, first discussed by Antoine-Nicolas Condorcet and Thomas Paine in the late eighteenth century, that poverty was the outcome of a social, not a natural, pattern and could be reduced and possibly eliminated outright through specific social policies was, in the words of historian Gareth Stedman Jones, "smothered at birth," and disregarded by both revolutionaries and moderates.[3] The neglect of these themes has had longlasting consequences, affecting economic and political debates even today.

ECONOMIC INEQUALITY

The concept of economic inequality refers to the distribution of resources among groups or individuals. Further, it implies that differences in income and wealth need to be qualified by some kind of value judgment. Hence, three elements are necessary to discuss economic inequality: a theory of distribution, a set of moral and legal norms that define what is "just" or "fair" (or at least acceptable), and data and statistical tools. We discuss the historical evolution of analytical techniques in the next chapter; here we discuss which theories of distribution characterized classical political economy and neoclassical thought.

One might expect that, because of its close connection to fundamental economic concepts such as income and wealth, inequality should also be at the core of economic analysis. Yet this is not the case: only in relatively recent times and only for a small cohort of researchers has inequality emerged as a powerful research subject. Why? After all, even if we were to accept the bizarre idea that economics is a value-free discipline, we could still discuss inequality, limiting our analysis to a theory of resource distribution while leaving values adjudication to moral philosophy. The theories of distribution developed by economists over time, however, are unsuitable for the study of inequality, and inequality has long remained on the margins of economics when not neglected altogether. In fact, whereas a theory of personal income and wealth distribution, which is vital to the study of inequality, has been prominently absent from the economics literature, another kind of distribution theory has played a very important role, namely, functional distribution.

Functional distribution considers what share of the aggregate income goes to each factor of production (that is, to each element that contributes to production). As much as inequality has traditionally been removed from the picture, to that same degree functional distribution has been conspicuous. Functional distribution is at the core of the analyses of classical economists such as Adam Smith, David Ricardo, and Karl Marx, and has survived in good health right up to the present.

In this chapter we discuss what distribution meant for classical and neoclassical economics and show how personal distribution and inequality were neglected as subjects of inquiry.

THE CLASSICAL ECONOMISTS

The roots of classical economic thought can be traced back to the Scottish Enlightenment in the second half of the eighteenth century. Beyond David Hume's 1752 *Essays* and Sir James Steuart's 1767 treatise *An Inquiry into the Principles of Political Oeconomy* (which introduced into English the term "political economy" from the title of a French book that was 150 years older: Antoine de Montchrétien's *Traicté de l'oeconomie politique* of 1616), the central work from this time was Adam Smith's *The Wealth of Nations*, first published in 1776. In the words of the historian of economic thought Roger Backhouse, Smith's *Wealth of Nations* "was inseparable from moral philosophy – from the project of seeking to find a basis on which people could live together when the Church no longer provided an unquestioned set of answers to questions about how society should be organized."[4] Finding the moral basis of a "good" society was Smith's project, a pursuit that had characterized the works of many authors before him, and he was able to combine moral philosophy with an analysis of how an economy and its institutions work.

In the first half of the nineteenth century, however, political economy tended to lose any relation to moral philosophy and to acquire a more "scientific" character. A key figure in this transition was Thomas R. Malthus, who in 1798 published his famous *Essay on the Principle of Population*. In it, Malthus still heavily relied on the framework of moral philosophy. The discussion, however, was presented as a scientific analysis, applying Newtonian principles to political issues.

Whereas Malthus still drew on both the old-style moral framework and the more contemporary scientific attitude, David Ricardo, a close friend of Malthus, achieved a full detachment from eighteenth-century moral philosophy. Ricardo's *On the Principles of Political Economy and Taxation* (1817) marked the apogee of the classical period in economics. He was followed by a number of important scholars, among them Jean-Baptiste Say, the two Mills (James and his son, John Stuart), William Senior, Robert Torrens, Henry Thornton, John Elliott Cairnes, and many others, including Karl Marx.[5] The publication of William Stanley Jevons's *Theory of Political Economy* in 1871 is conventionally considered to inaugurate a different epoch, when economics would become professionalized and increasingly formalized through the prominent use of mathematics: the neoclassical economic thought.

Differing from the post-1870s economists, who were highly professionalized and mostly full-time academics, the classical economists were highly varied in educational background and profession. Smith and Malthus were academics. Ricardo and James Mill were active in politics and members of Parliament, while others were civil servants or belonged to the professions. Their formal education tended to be in the classics, philosophy, mathematics, or law, which perhaps explains their ability to deal with an extensive range of issues. Their beliefs were rooted in Jeremy Bentham's utilitarianism, strongly egalitarian and individualist. None of them retreated from merging analytical propositions with policy implications, and all were particularly vocal in political debates on matters such as the Corn Laws, trade protectionism, colonial affairs, and the poor-laws system. Their approach and their discipline were (and are) called "political economy" rather than "economics" precisely because they were concerned with the interaction between the economic and the political dimensions. It was not until 1890, with the publication of Alfred Marshall's *Principles of Economics,* that the focus shifted to economics as a subject in its own right.

Despite a passion for the political economy of current problems, these authors never considered the problem of inequality to be of interest. Though seemingly a "political economy" theme par excellence, inequality among individuals never caught the attention of the classical political economists. The historical context and intellectual environment in which they lived, discussed in the next section, were not conducive to such an inquiry.

DISTRIBUTION IN CLASSICAL POLITICAL ECONOMY

The classical economists' historical context lies between tradition, as exemplified by the natural law philosophers and the physiocrats of the late eighteenth century, and innovation, the changing world of the Industrial Revolution.

On the one hand, economics was considered part of moral philosophy growing out of the natural law system, which held that people maximized their overall welfare through pursuing self-interest. On the other hand, the attention of the physiocrats – the eighteenth-century French economists who believed that the wealth of a nation was derived from the value of its agriculture – to the different roles of landlords, farmers, and manufacturers in a country's economy seemed to call for a theory of distribution. The determination of the "natural" level of wage, rent, and profit that goes toward forming the "natural" price – the classical Smithian theory of distribution – comes from there.

Moreover, the Industrial Revolution, occurring between the mid-1700s and the mid-1800s, created one of the greatest explosions of economic growth in the history of humankind, with a sustained increase in population and the development of a middle class in Western economies. Notwithstanding the huge growth in population, per capita gross domestic product (GDP) grew without abating. In those times, the interest could not be in any topic other than production – and specifically industrial production, since agriculture was already starting its secular decline – and its distribution in terms of profits, wages, and rents to the factors of production, respectively capital, labour, and land. In Ricardo's words, "To determine the laws which regulate this distribution is the principal problem in Political Economy."[6] The concern was to understand and explain such a chaotically growing world.

Thus, the distribution of production, central to the classical economic thought, is "functional" since it pertains to the distribution of the product to the groups that contribute to production. The societal focus shifted from social status to economic criteria, and in place of groupings such as priests, knights, and commoners, a new social stratification created by the Industrial Revolution – the social classes – appeared.

Irrespective of the massive economic and social changes

brought about by the Industrial Revolution, however, inequality never attracted the interest of the classical economists. Even when they dealt with taxation issues, as they did frequently, the aim was to evaluate the effects on production without consideration for equity. Where a reference to equity is present, as in Ricardo's discussion of the ability-to-pay (that is, the taxation issue), the interest is on the overall economic growth of the nation. Taxation was exclusively a way to support the state and its activities – the wealth of nations – and not a way to promote equality (as the preference of the classical economists for indirect taxation also suggests). Even on a hot topic like the population problem – the population was increasing in a geometrical ratio while subsistence was increasing only in an arithmetical ratio – worries about (in)equality were absent. The Ricardian minimum-of-existence – what is necessary to workers to subsist and to perpetuate humankind – reflects the same idea.

Intellectuals of the time did not address explicitly and consistently the presence and meaning of economic inequality in the life of individuals. Some were rich and some were poor – that was simply a fact of life. Apart from Marx, economists never asked why some were *so* rich and some *so* poor, and Marx did not develop a theory of personal distribution, limiting himself to providing a different theory for functional distribution – a theory that was "mere froth on the surface of the waves," as Cannan remarked.[7]

Though class stratification in eighteenth- and early nineteenth-century society, combined with low interclass mobility, might render the income of a class a good approximation to the individual incomes within that class, this was not why personal distribution was disregarded. More simply, inequality was not on the conceptual horizon of those who reflected on the functioning of society. Even during the French Revolution, the bourgeoisie favored political equality but not social or economic equality. The time was not ripe for a social revolution that would make the individual its center. Much time would elapse before the individual became the true focus of societal studies.

THE MARGINALIST REVOLUTION

From about 1870 on, a great change took place in economic theory: the "marginalist" revolution, based on marginal utility and individual maximization.[8] As Thorstein Veblen (speaking about Alfred Marshall) called them later, the proponents of this revolution are known as "the neoclassical economists."

By the start of the 1900s, this was *the* economics. Unlike classical thought, which was mainly British, this new stream in economic thought emerged in a number of distinct areas: England, Austria, France, Sweden, Italy, and, later and with increasing relevance, the United States. The first products of this new phase, according to a large consensus, are William Stanley Jevons's *Theory of Political Economy* and Carl Menger's *Principles of Economics,* both published in 1871. The height of the neoclassical theory was reached with *Éléments d'économie politique pure* (*Elements of Pure Economics*), by Léon Walras, published in 1874, and Alfred Marshall's *Principles of Economics,* published in 1890.[9] A huge number of additional contributions followed, forming a conceptual corpus that evolved over time into what modern economics is today. All textbooks in microeconomics (and many in macroeconomics) still rely on the same basic principles enunciated by the neoclassical school.

In contradistinction to the classical school, the leading exponents of neoclassical economics were almost all academics. They specialized in economics and made it a discipline, moving it away from political philosophy and toward mathematics and "science," thus shaping its future permanently.

DISTRIBUTION IN NEOCLASSICAL ECONOMICS

The period extending from the late 1800s to the First World War was still a time of rapid growth, characterized by the spread of industrialization and scientific progress. Social and economic development, as well as overwhelming advancements in technology, made classical thought old-fashioned and, in certain important respects, outdated. The rentiers had lost their importance and were disappearing as a leading class. The very concept of class was less clear, and the term itself was progressively vanishing from the economic lexicon. The more neutral term "group" – whether composed of producers or of consumers – was replacing it, and the "representative agent" became the key subject of new economic theorizing.

Production is at the core of economics, and the pricing of resources is the most conspicuous problem dealt with by economics. The focus of the neoclassical economists was still on the functional distribution of income, though within a different theoretical framework: a theory that explained distribution according to the concept of (marginal) productivity. Since productivity, the contribution of a specific factor to production, is the benchmark for the reward, the earnings cannot be equal because productivity is not equal across groups (or across people, as the theory later evolved). The neoclassical theory of production sees the market as a way to obtain optimal resource allocation, and the neoclassical theory of distribution does not have any normative suggestion as to how much should accrue to each factor of production besides a simple cost comparison. This theory of distribution is incidental to the pricing process. Whereas in the classical school, Dobb held, "income-distribution is treated as being the result of social institutions (e.g. property-ownership) and social relations," in the neoclassical school "it is determined by the conditions of exchange. In the one case it is determined from outside and in the other case from inside the process of market prices."[10]

Though we might consider the array of market rewards as the basis for a theory of personal distribution, inequality was not yet a concern. The functional distribution was still at the core, and the focus was still on the distributive shares, or how much of the overall income goes to every factor of production. The difference with respect to the past is that the different income shares that go to each factor of production were by the neoclassical school determined technically through a production function. First fully formulated by Philip Wicksteed in 1894, and culminating in the Cobb-Douglas function of the 1920s, the production function became the hallmark of the neoclassical theory of distribution and is still among the unavoidable tools of economists.[11] As Dobb summarized the general attitude toward distributional issues at that time, "Questions of property-ownership or class relations and conflicts were regarded as falling outside the economist's domain, not directly affecting, in major respects at least, the phenomena and relations with which economic analysis was properly concerned, and belonging instead to the province of the economic historian or the sociologist."[12]

Paradoxically, both classical and neoclassical economics share the same sin: they refer to an archetypical individual, who has in fact no subjectivity at all. Neoclassical theory rests on the concept of the individual as a representative agent, while classical economic theory is based on the concept of class, in which all individuals are implicitly equal, being leveled by the same economic condition. The representative agent of neoclassical economics is what he does, a consumer or a producer, whereas the member of a class in the previous decades was what he owned: work, capital, and land. By definition, in both approaches there is not yet space for a complete theory of personal distribution because there is no *person*. Here again, as in classical economics, the issues were other: the business cycle, research methods – which resulted in increasing mathematization – and the concern for providing an empirical basis to theory. This was the economics of the first half of the twentieth century.

WELFARE ECONOMICS: A NEOCLASSICAL OPENING TO PERSONAL INCOME DISTRIBUTION

It would be incorrect to say that personal income distribution was completely absent from the neoclassical landscape. The welfare economics of the first half of the twentieth century and the flourishing empirical and statistical research of the middle decades of that century were major drivers of an approach to personal income distribution.

From the early twentieth century on, a parallel research effort directed toward the personal distribution of income began to develop. This new interest stemmed from the socialist wave at the end of the nineteenth century, whose effects were accepted by many influential economists and not disregarded by the most influential of them all, Alfred Marshall. Thus in England a concept of welfare began to form, together with some considerations – not foreign to the classical economists – on when and how society should admit state intervention. Social welfare was primarily measured as the sum of individual utilities (the utility function, which expresses utility as a function of the amount of goods consumed, is the pillar of neoclassical theorizing), an approach pioneered by Bentham and shared by most influential economists. Since income distribution can be observed in terms of either market income (how the original incomes, generated in the market, are distributed among the earners) or disposable income (the distribution of market incomes, adjusted by taxes and transfers), theorizing about state intervention was from the very beginning intertwined with the theme of social justice. Inequality in distribution and personal and societal welfare became subjects that economists could not disregard.

This welfare concern became widely present in the economic literature of the first few decades of the twentieth century, especially thanks to the work of Alfred Cecil Pigou and Hugh Dalton. As Dalton put it, "While studying economics at Cambridge in 1909–10 ... distribution as between persons was either left out of the textbooks altogether or treated so briefly as to suggest that it raised no question, which could not be answered either by generalizations about the factors of production, or by plodding statistical investigations, which professors of economic theory were content to leave to lesser men."[13]

Dalton's interest was primarily in the measurement of income inequality, still within a fully utilitarian perspective relying on Pigou's transfer principle. The theoretical basis of this principle was still the law of diminishing marginal utility, assessing that the more one has of anything, the less is the increase in utility of one additional unit. However, the Pigouvian translation in terms of redistribution was that a (mean-preserving) transfer of income from a richer person to an identical poorer person would increase the aggregate utility (provided that utility is identical for all persons). Dalton broadened this principle, relating it to aggregate welfare: "If a given income is to be distributed among a given number of persons, it is evident that economic welfare will be a maximum when all incomes are equal."[14] The only argument against complete equality, in this case, may emerge only when an attempt to achieve it causes a reduction in total income (which is exactly the evergreen thesis that equality damages growth).

This position – highly egalitarian, and as such rather unpalatable – was seriously questioned by Lionel Robbins on the basis of the noncomparability of utilities.[15] Pareto in 1906 had already rejected cardinal utilities and additive utility functions (that is, the idea that it was actually possible to measure utility), opening the way to the ordinalist view of the social welfare function (the idea that instead, it is only possible to simply rank utilities). What Robbins added is the subtler statement that their additivity is just an assumption, thus cutting egalitarianism out of the scientific realm of economics and relegating it to politics or philosophy.[16] With this devastating methodological critique, the "new" welfare economics began. As Dobb incisively summarized:

> [The] older (Pigouvian) writing about Welfare had derived from the "Law of Diminishing Utility" the principle that the less unequally a given national product was distributed, ceteris paribus, the greater the resulting total sum of utility or welfare would be. Such pronounced egalitarian conclusions were manifestly unwelcome and embarrassing in certain quarters. It seemed a relief to have a system of welfare economics from which awkward questions about distribution could be excluded; and the "New" Welfare Economics (priding itself on its rigorous positivism) proceeded to refashion itself in such a way as to make the intrusion of such questions irrelevant and unnecessary.[17]

This welfare doctrine blossomed, focusing on the problem of the efficient allocation of resources in the form of so-called Pareto optimality, according to which an allocation is Pareto optimal whenever it cannot be reorganized so to improve the condition (utility) of somebody without worsening that of others. Efficiency was legitimated as *the* economic principle, while equity was de facto marginalized. This is precisely the reason why Amartya Sen repeatedly affirms in his works that the Pareto conditions are actually unfitting a social optimum: "If the lot of the poor cannot be made any better without cutting into the affluence of the rich, the situation would be Pareto optimal despite the disparity between the rich and the poor ... The almost single-minded concern of modern welfare economics with Pareto optimality does not make that engaging branch of study particularly suitable for investigating problems of inequality."[18] It is noteworthy that Sen does not accept the "old" welfare economics either, claiming that the use of an overall social welfare function is not the right way to measure inequality.[19]

From the 1930s on, the principle that economics is and must be a value-free science would remain dominant, and the non-accidental supremacy of statistics in handling inequality (or, more precisely, the dispersion of earnings) helped economics disregard it.

Atkinson, sharing Sen's position, asserted the inconsistency of talking about economic policy without having an idea of social welfare that is different from both the old utilitarianism and the new Pareto dominance. He seemed to indicate that, in order to reach a sound welfare theory able to study phenomena such as inequality, the statistical and philosophical discussions of the 1970s should be merged.[20] In some way, income distribution had to be "brought in from the cold," both for itself as a moral stance and as a practical issue for coping with current huge economic disparities. Value judgments and an ethical basis are essential for policy evaluation and for tackling economic inequality, a discussion of which must inevitably refer to ethical and moral principles. This is, however, a long shot. As Robert Solow stated in his 1998 Tanner Lecture: "A lecture on human values by an economist: one might as well invite a turkey buzzard to lecture on table manners: how would the poor beast know where to start?"[21]

BEYOND WELFARE ECONOMICS

Welfare considerations aside, the idea that income disparity among individuals is obvious – and so can be considered normal – was commonly accepted by neoclassical economists. The central tenets of the logic behind the existence of income disparity were (1) that individuals are diverse by nature, and their differences in endowment can be evaluated differently by society depending on the productive context and consumer tastes, and (2) that individuals are the main determinants of their own destiny, and though wealth comes from "nature" (or inheritance), it also comes from personal attitudes and the propensity to accept risk in the first instance. The most relevant academic contribution to this approach is undoubtedly Milton Friedman's famous 1953 article, "Choice, Chance and the Personal Distribution of Income." In his view, individuals are fundamentally diverse by nature and endowments and "inequality of income in a society may be regarded ... as a reflection of a deliberate choice in accordance with the tastes and preferences of the members of the society."[22] This is how the "cold" theory of choice under uncertainty monopolized the "hot" problem of income distribution. Nothing – or very little – is said in the literature of the time about inequality in the distribution of the ownership of capital. Apparently, only Nobel laureate James Meade addressed the issue, in 1964, by stating that the dominance of technical progress would penalize labour income in favor of capital income, and that in turn would increase the overall inequality, as capital income is more unequally distributed than labour income.[23] Only in 2013 – fifty years or two generations hence – would Thomas Piketty put the role of wealth in generating inequality again at the core of the inequality debate.[24]

Certain exogenous factors, such as the mating between people of the same class or the rules for inheritances, may even accelerate the trend of increasing inequality. In 1975 a second contribution by Meade appeared in which he considered all the possible circumstances that generate or perpetuate inequality. He discussed factors of fortune ("the basic structural endowments of genes, property, education, and social contacts") and factors of luck ("the many chances in life which determine the actual outcomes within these structures of basic endowments") to tentatively conclude that "fortune is not quite so secondary to luck." This conclusion was conducive to focusing socially on the "luck" factors with policy action so as to counterbalance the "fortune" factors.[25]

Another important characteristic of those mid-century studies was a new focus on actual data collection. Friedman himself in 1953 recalled that his theoretical outcomes fit the observed patterns, an empirical issue on which he had earlier worked along with his colleague Simon Kuznets – a leading researcher in the inequality area and a protagonist of the empirical research agenda of the 1940s and 1950s (we discuss him more at length in chapter 3). What were these observed patterns?

Aggregate data on income distribution show two characteristics: dispersion and asymmetry. Dispersion simply means that incomes are different from person to person: people fall into several income classes, and some people have low incomes, some have high incomes, and some are in between. Each income class has in general a different density of people in it: usually this density is higher in the low- and middle-income classes and lower in the high-income class. Asymmetry means that these income classes are not symmetrically located on both sides of the median value of income (that level of income that stays exactly in the middle of a distribution) but are preponderantly located on its left side. In other words, income distribution tends to cluster to the left of both the median and the mean income: the majority of persons have an income lower than the median or the mean income (see figure 2.1). The poor are many and the (very) rich are few.

During the entire mid-twentieth century and even later, the neoclassical theory of distribution focused on the natural distribution of abilities, on rational choice theory, and on uncertainty and risk as a way to explain dispersion and asymmetry.[26] No great success, however, crowned it.

DISTRIBUTION IN TWENTIETH-CENTURY ECONOMICS

Personal distribution found space in neither Keynes, nor Sraffa, nor other important authors of the twentieth century. Keynes, for instance, believed that "there is social and psychological justification for significant inequalities of incomes and wealth."[27] Beyond that, Nicholas Kaldor reminds us, "Keynes ... was never interested in the problem of distribution as such."[28] In fact, Keynes discussed it only tangentially, in reference to the "euthanasia of the rentier" (the functionless investor, as he labels him), destined to disappear once capital has become as abundant as to almost nullify its return. Yet in the 1930s, the story of distribution was still mainly functional, as if once it is determined what goes to the different factors of production (whether through the market

Figure 2.1. A typical personal income distribution

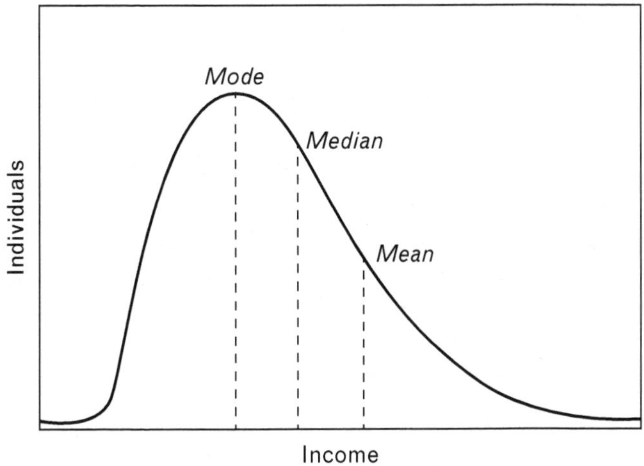

mechanism or class struggle), the issue of how much these factors earn with respect to each other leaves the territory of economics and enters the arena of ethics, philosophy, and law.

Goldfarb and Leonard found that the American Economic Association's 1946 *Readings in the Theory of Income Distribution* included thirty-one (out of thirty-two) papers in which distribution was conceived as functional. Though they noticed an increasing interest in the personal distribution of income in the publications of the National Bureau of Economic Research (NBER) during the 1940s and 1950s, the main discussion was more about data availability than interpretation.[29] Those were the years in which the empirical side of the personal distribution problem was approached with almost complete detachment from theory. Obviously, nobody denies the importance of sophisticated tools for handling a complex topic. However, as we will suggest in chapter 3, this technical "drift" contributed to the dismissal of the subject of personal distribution in economics.

In fact, three important conferences on distribution in the 1960s, which saw the participation of the most prominent economists of the time, still testify to the lack of any substantive theory of the size distribution of revenues. The three conferences are the 1961 and 1967 NBER conferences and the 1964 IEA (International Economic Association) conference, the papers of which were published in 1964, 1969, and 1968, respectively. Tibor Scitovsky's survey article on the 1961 NBER conference highlighted the large number of theories on the functional distribution of income and the variety of approaches applied to an equally great variety of phenomena.[30] He found nothing on the personal distribution.

Regrettably, at least for the construction of a theory of size distribution of revenues, twentieth-century economics has been occupied in diatribes between the two competing Keynesian and neoclassical theories, leaving no space for other ideas or for contamination from other disciplines, such as sociology and politics. Thus, in the absence of a developed theory on the size distribution of income, "there are a good many bits and pieces of theory lying around in the literature that can, with a little trimming of edges, be fitted into a mosaic called 'The Theory of Income Size Distribution.'"[31]

Ten years later, Atkinson reviewed the contents of articles published in the *Economic Journal* over the preceding fifty-year period and noticed a dearth of papers on why the connection between income inequality and the most debated macroeconomic variables – for instance, the economic performance of a country – were still unstudied, and why there was only scant inquiry into how theory can explain what accrues to the single individual.[32] These questions are still unanswered since the focus has remained on how to enlarge the pie rather than on reconsidering the size of its slices. The theory of personal income distribution stands out as the most notable victim of this paradigm that has dominated economics – a paradigm whereby the liberal philosophy and the focus on production do not admit inequality in distribution.

Thus it is widely agreed among economists that even today there is no uniform theory of the personal distribution of income. The textbook explanation (if and when textbooks address this issue) rests on globalization and technical change, separately or in conjunction. According to this view, the different pace of education – which increases the supply of skilled labour – and of technological change – which augments the demand for skilled labour – would cause wage dispersion, also strengthened by globalization.[33] However, what happens in the top part of the income distribution – that part where the rich and super-rich are – is not in tune with this hypothesis. The skill-bias explanation has little to say, for instance, about why the earnings of the very very rich (0.01 per cent of the population) have increased relative to those of the very rich (0.1 per cent) and the rich (1 per cent). Factors such as globalization and technological change may operate through the remuneration of top executives or through the rents earned by "superstars," but actually, as Atkinson states, very few models exist that offer convincing explanations, and unfortunately, they do not seem to be easily testable.[34] Moreover, in the top part of the distribution there are both labour incomes (the working rich) and capital incomes (both working rich and rentiers), and it is not clear to what degree they are separate groups. Manageable models that bring the two income sources together do not exist. "An overall framework is missing," Atkinson writes, and "the economic analysis of the distribution of income is in need of further development."[35]

Similarly, there is no uniform theory for inequality, inequality being nothing else than a nonuniform personal distribution of income (and wealth). Surprisingly, and scarcely recalled, the presence of a theory of inequality per parts mirrors an interesting and nonconformist judgment by Schumpeter on the absence of a classical full theory of distribution: "What people meant by theory of distribution ... was a compound of separate theories of profits, rent, and wages, each of which was based on a distinct principle of its own."[36]

Nor is there even a bridge between the functional and the personal sides of distribution, as two otherwise distant scholars such as Friedman and Atkinson point out. Friedman's statement, "This absence of ... a theoretical bridge connecting the functional distribution of income with the personal distribution is a major gap in modern economic theory," is echoed by Atkinson's: "The factor-distribution is certainly part of the story, but it is only part, and the other links in the chain need to receive attention."[37] Unfortunately, drawing inferences about personal distribution starting from the functional distribution, while it might have been reasonable in past centuries, is now hazardous. In fact, any strong correspondence between types of incomes and classes of persons is lost in our time, and even constant income shares can hide wide movements within them, generating income dispersion. Today, some wage and salary earners (the so-called working rich) can enjoy a significant amount of income, and property income is a more diffused reality than in the past. Thus the overlapping of types of income and classes of persons (which prima facie might justify a focus on functional distribution in order to infer something of the personal one) is increasingly loose.[38]

THREE

The Statistical Drift of Inequality Studies

> A concept of inequality is normative or is not. Hence, when we speak of inequality, we speak either of dispersion or of injustice.
>
> Serge-Christophe Kolm, as quoted by Peter Lambert[1]

Around the turn of the twentieth century, great changes took place in Western societies. The mixing of income sources, one of the new economic aspects of the changing world, brought to the surface unprecedented perspectives. The old, clear social connotations of owning *just* land, *just* capital, or *just* labour (and so being just landlords, capitalists, or workers) gradually ceased to exist, and the theory of distribution could no longer be consistently identified with the theory of production. Since economic theory had almost nothing to offer as an explanation of how social income is distributed among *individuals,* factual observation was the only remedy for this deficiency, and statistics appeared to be the right medicine. Thus, at the peak of the neoclassical thought, the first important and systematic observation of the characteristics of the size distribution of income took place. The scholar who worked that fundamental switch was Vilfredo Pareto.

PARETO'S α

Vilfredo Pareto (1848–1923) was an Italian-French nobleman, engineer, and industrial manager before becoming a scholar of economics and sociology and obtaining the chair in economics at Lausanne, where he succeeded the famous Léon Walras. Pareto was – though not without ambiguities – an ultraliberal intellectual. Yet he recognized the role of a collectivist state in leading the economy to an equilibrium,[2] and, while still defending freedom of the press and of teaching, was close to the Italian dictator Mussolini and applauded him as entirely fit to restore order to Italian society. Pareto is universally known for his concept of the maximum of society's "ophelimity," or economic satisfaction. This is the famous *Pareto optimality* principle, which has traditionally played a significant role in research on welfare economics (we mentioned it in chapter 2 in the section titled "Welfare Economics: A Neoclassical Opening to Personal Income Distribution"). Here we address only Pareto's law of distribution, or Pareto's α.

What did Pareto do? He simply interpreted a set of empirical observations in order to understand whether wealth distribution depended primarily on the structure of the economy, on human nature, or perhaps just on chance.[3] Operationally, he examined fiscal data at various points in time for Great Britain and Ireland, Prussia and the Kingdom of Saxony, the Swiss canton of Vaud, a sample of Italian municipalities, and the cities of Basel in Switzerland and Augsburg in Germany. In all these sites he found empirical proof that the distribution of revenues (Pareto's word is *richesse*, "wealth") could be approximated by the following equation:

$$\log N = \log A - \alpha \log X,$$

where X is a given income and N the number of individuals with income equal to or greater than X (A is a constant that we do not need to discuss here). This is the equation of a downward-sloping straight line. Its logarithmic form implies that the slope α represents the percentage variation in N (the number of individuals) following a given percentage variation in X (the given income). Thus, as income increases by some percentage points, the proportion of people with more than that income decreases by some percentage points: the increasingly rich become increasingly fewer. Increasingly fewer by how much? As much as the value of α indicates.

Remarkably, Pareto found α to be relatively constant over space and time: in particular, α turned out to be around 1.5 – the value for the United Kingdom in 1843 – ranging from a minimum of 1.24 (Basel in 1887) to a maximum of 1.89 (Prussia in 1852). As Pareto commented, "It is absolutely impossible that these results are the outcome of chance."[4]

Even more important was Pareto's conclusion at the very end of the *Cours*. In a chapter titled "La physiologie sociale," he stated that unequal distribution depended on "the very nature of individuals"[5] rather than on any structural characteristic of society. Even deep changes in the organization of society would have but a slight influence in modifying the distribution.

Presenting his analysis based on empirical observation with all the chrisms of scientific inquiry, Pareto was actually formulating a theory of society that could easily become the foundation of a conservative political manifesto. According to his research, the distribution of wealth is not determined by the economic structure of society and institutions but by the distribution of certain natural qualities among individuals. It was easy to interpret α as an inequality measure, as Pareto did, but the substantial obscurity of α and its ultimately incorrect interpretation were not as easy to detect. A vivid debate followed Pareto's discovery of this "law," animated by prominent statisticians and economists, such as Arthur Lyon Bowley, Felice Vinci, Raffaele D'Addario, Luigi Amoroso, Francis Ysidro Edgeworth, Arthur Cecil Pigou, and Costantino Bresciani-Turroni.

Bresciani-Turroni, in particular, was the scholar who put the tombstone on Pareto's α after it became clear that something was still needed in order to explain income inequality. That something was the concept of concentration, that is, how many persons as a percentage of the entire population had that percentage income, instead of just how many persons had a specific income. In 1939 Bresciani-Turroni published an article in which he kindly thanked Pareto for his meaningful insights into the income distribution while suggesting at the same time that the data did not always support Pareto's α.[6] Pareto's α thus ceased to be considered an indicator of inequality.

However, as long as Pareto's α and "Pareto's distribution" played the roles, respectively, of the inequality measure and the distribution function par excellence, a huge amount of work (data, calculation, indices, observations) was undertaken by early twentieth-century statisticians in Pareto's steps. In fact, to speak about inequality in distribution it is necessary first to have some idea of the functional form of the distribution itself, since inequality is the by-product of the dispersion (how far the observations are from the mean of the distribution) and asymmetry (how different the form of the distribution is on the two sides of the median, that is, its central value). Thus Pareto's story and all that followed might help explain the absence of a meaningful theory about income distribution because Pareto had offered a theory, though a computational one, and a lot of effort had to be devoted to improving and advancing it. Those were the years during which the famous Italian school of statistics produced many important technical advances suggesting alternative indices to Pareto's α. Benini, Mortara, Cantelli, D'Addario, Amoroso, and others worked particularly on the right-hand tail of the distribution (see figure 2.1 in chapter 2) to formulate the best "power law" able to approximate its actual values for the very rich.[7] But more important, the idea of concentration – absent until then – started to percolate through income distribution studies.

Within this new conceptual framework, two independent and important contributions appeared in the early twentieth century that were destined to change forever the debate and to pave the way for an enormous and fruitful body of research on the theory and application of statistical measures: the Lorenz curve, introduced in 1905, and the Gini index, introduced in 1914.

LORENZ'S DIAGRAM

Max Otto Lorenz was an American economist and statistician of German ancestry who taught at the University of Wisconsin for a few years and then became chief statistician at the Interstate Commerce Commission. His date of birth is uncertain, although he was certainly born in the second half of the 1870s. Though he died after an apparently inconspicuous life as a civil servant, the curve that bears his name has become one of the best-known and widely used tools in the statistician's tool box. As Lorenz put it, the purpose of his 1905 article – apparently his only publication in a scientific journal – appeared to be rather humble: to discuss some techniques used thus far in distribution analysis, and to suggest "an additional one" in order to "take account simultaneously of changes in wealth and changes in population." In particular, Lorenz insisted on the benefits that a graphical representation of distributional data would offer: "The method is as follows: plot along one axis cumulated per cent of the population from poorest to richest, and along the other the per cent of the total wealth held by these per cents of the population." Because 100 per cent is the maximum value on both axes, the graph is a square, and the 45-degree straight line drawn from the origin – the diagonal of the square – represents equal distributions. In fact, every point on the diagonal individuates an equal pair of cumulated values (the *x* per cent of total population owns an equal *x* per cent of total wealth), which means that each individual owns the same amount of wealth. "With an unequal distribution the curves will always begin and end in the same points as with an equal distribution, but they will be bent in the middle; and the rule of interpretation will be, as the bow is bent, concentration increases."[8]

In other words, inequality is present when every chosen upper-income group (deciles, quintiles, or other) of the population receives more than its perfect equality share and every low-income group receives less than that. Therefore, the inequality curve lies below (or to the right of) the 45-degree line, and the more it lies below (or the more it bends toward the right side of the diagram), the more unequal is the distribution of revenues (or wealth, as Lorenz says, or income) among the population. It is worth noting that the statistical definition of inequality results from the statistical concept of equality, as in moral philosophy.

As far as we know, the diagram – somewhat different from Lorenz's original 1905 one – was called the Lorenz curve only in

1912, by Willford I. King.[9] Lorenz's curve then received the final consecration by Corrado Gini in 1914 when, speaking of his concentration ratio *R*, destined to become the Gini coefficient, Gini claimed that Lorenz's graphical method was a suitable way for representing it geometrically.[10] From then on, that concentration curve was the Lorenz curve.

THE GINI INDEX

Corrado Gini (1884–1965) came from the Italian agrarian high bourgeoisie and had a definite conservative political profile. He was a highly versatile scholar, contributing to a number of fields, including statistics, economics, demography, sociology, and anthropology, and he is universally known today as the father of the most famous index of inequality, the Gini index.[11] We will return later to the properties that make it one of the most widely used measures in modern statistical work on distribution.

In 1939 Gini edited a compilation in Italian of several of his writings completed between 1909 and 1914, when he was working extensively on concentration.[12] In this volume, two measures representing two different steps in his conceptual elaboration are present: the index δ and the index *R*. Gini firstly elaborates δ for measuring the phenomenon of wealth concentration and, contrary to Pareto's outcome of a uniform distribution of wealth across countries and time, he found that total income distribution differs geographically. In a later and more important contribution, Gini elaborated the concentration ratio *R*, adding that it too can be obtained from the Lorenz curve.[13] The ratio *R* became what is commonly known as the Gini index. Although a more detailed discussion is available in the appendix to this book, it is worthwhile listing its major qualities here. First, being a ratio, it has the advantage of immediate comparability across groups. Also, it is independent from the mean value of the distribution (if the mean value changes without any change in the form of the distribution, the index does not change); it enjoys a scale and population independence (if every income is multiplied by a constant – that is, if the same population is evenly richer – and respectively, if every income is repeated *k* times – that is, if the population is *k* times larger – the index does not change); and it obeys the Pigouvian transfer principle (if income is transferred from a rich person to a poor person, the resulting distribution is more equal).

However, the Gini index, like other measures of inequality, also suffers from a number of drawbacks: (1) it considers only one dimension of inequality (a feature common, however, to the great majority of measures); (2) it is influenced by the thinness of the chosen unit;[14] (3) it reacts more to transfers around the mode – that is, the value that appears most often in a set of data – than to transfers to the extremes (the tails) of the distribution; (4) it does not obey the principle of exact decomposition into the two classic manifestations of inequality: within a group (of individuals, countries, or other) and between groups; and (5) it does not offer any information on the asymmetry of the distribution (economies with the same Gini index value can have very different distributions) since it is not able to identify where the rise (or fall) in income concentration occurs. This means that it may remain unchanged even as the distribution changes significantly as a consequence of redistributive forces working in different directions at different points. In this respect, we might say that the Gini index offers an opaque reading of the concentration in a distribution.

A BIFURCATION: INDICES AND DISTRIBUTIONS

Some important statistical research followed Gini's elaboration of his index during the twentieth century.

In one major line of work, scholars inquired how to interpret the characteristics of distributions and eventually how to capture their "inequality": is it dispersion, asymmetry, or concentration? Throughout the entire twentieth century statisticians worked incessantly in this subfield of distribution with the goal of defining the properties of a *good* index, and many indices, all with their own pros and cons, have been developed. There are measures of variation (or dispersion), such as the variance, the coefficient of variation, the relative mean deviation, and the entropy indices,[15] among which the most famous is the Theil index, developed by the University of Chicago econometrician Henri Theil. The main reason for its success is that this index is *exactly* decomposable into a between component and a within component: how much of the inequality is due to differences showed by the groups of observations in relation to each other and how much, conversely, is due to differences within each group of observations. Further measures refer to the skewness (or asymmetry), and others are simply derived from the empirical laws of income distribution, such as shares: how much a specific fraction of population receives, compared to the total population. Again, we discuss shares further in the appendix to this book.

In parallel, the interest in giving a theoretical explanation to the entire distribution was still vivid. In fact, along with data becoming increasingly available, a peculiar form of the empirical income distribution started to emerge, as we showed in figure 2.1 of chapter 2. This form exhibits a positive skewness – that is, a significant hump coincident with the mode of the distribution positioned to the left of both the median and the mean income – and a long right-hand tail: a hyperbola. In other words, data were disclosing that the great majority of people had – on average across (developed) countries – an income that was less than the mean income, whereas very few people had high incomes. These peculiar aspects were formally intriguing since Pareto's analytical expression was a hyperbola and as such it still had a role, though applicable to the tail only, that is, to the high-income case. Figure 3.1 shows three examples of this generalized form of the empirical distribution, with different dispersions around the mean (different values of the parameter σ). The solid line shows that many people have an income around the mean income (a more egalitarian distribution), while the other two distributions, indicated by the dashed lines, show increasingly greater dispersion of incomes (they are thus less egalitarian).

A FURTHER BIFURCATION: ANALYTICAL OR THEORETICAL INTERPRETATIONS?

Not unexpectedly, research on the theory of distribution was affected by this complex empirical evidence and was increasingly close to an impasse: either the theoretical explanation fit only a portion of the empirical distribution, its right hand tail, or the mathematical and statistical expression of the entire distribution were unable to offer any theoretical explanation of it.

Scholarly work seemed to show that the best candidate for representing the entire distribution of revenues was the log-normal distribution: a statistical distribution normal in the logarithms. In other words, a logarithmic transformation of a normal distribution that has the nice property of moving the mode away from the mean – precisely, to its left.[16] This results from the mathematical

Figure 3.1. Three different log-normal distributions

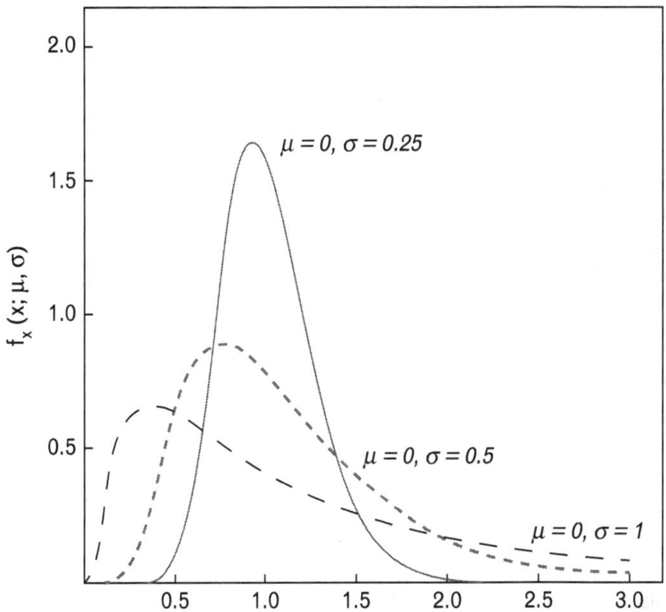

property of logarithms of emphasizing the incomes at the bottom of the distribution (to the left of the mean) since the lower the incomes, the greater is their logarithmic difference. Thus, around the middle of the twentieth century it was agreed that the great majority of observed distributions might conform in their right-hand tail – that is, for high income levels – to the Pareto distribution (a hyperbola), while over their remaining range they are better represented by a log-normal distribution fatter in the tails, called "leptokurtic" distributions (as the three curves in figure 3.1). Not surprisingly, as mentioned just before, for a smaller σ (the dispersion) the distribution is more equal, insofar as it is more centered around its mean income. In lay terms, the majority of the population has on average the same income.

This statistical work prompted further questions. Why is the distribution concentrated on the left of a function that is asymmetrical, with a longer right-hand tail? In technical terms, why is the most common income level (the mode of the distribution) typically less than halfway up the distribution, while the income halfway up the distribution (the median of the distribution) is below the mean of the distribution? In lay terms again, in a "typical" society most people have an income that is lower than the mean, and only a few people have incomes that are higher, and often much higher, than the mean. Why?

To explain such empirical evidence, some scholars relied on a stochastic process as the principal force, in which the observed pattern is entirely attributable to chance. Income level at time t depends uniquely on its value at time $t-1$ *plus* an independent stochastic variable normally distributed, that is, with zero mean and constant variance (that is, its distance from the mean). In technical terms, the change in income is a *random variable*. Depending on the assumption about the random term, and using a mathematical theorem known as the central limit theorem,[17] we can state whether the income distributes as a normal curve (like those shown in figure 3.2) or as a log-normal curve (like those shown in figure 3.1). If the random term (u) is additive, that is, if it is added to last period income (y_t) to give this period income (y_{t+1}), such as $y_{t+1} = y_t + u_t$, we will have a normal distribution. If the random term is multiplicative, such as $y_{t+1} = y_t u_t$, the outcome will be a log-normal distribution.

This abstract inquiry, however, does not provide much substance. As Harold Lydall has written, "These theories rely too much on the stochastic element and too little on the economic and social factors underlying the distribution of income."[18]

Figure 3.2. Three different normal (Gaussian) distributions

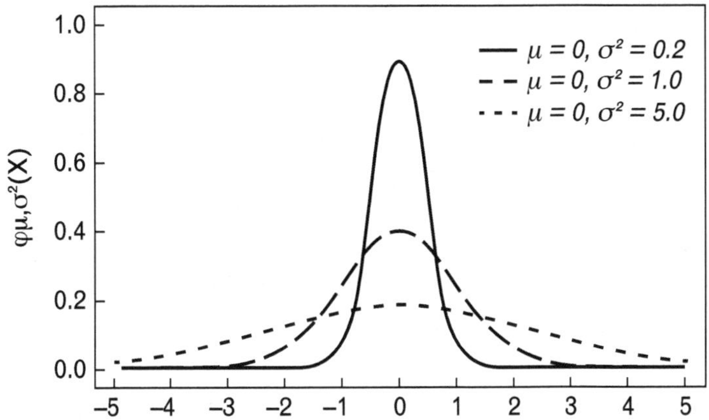

Among the theories that are centered on such economic and social factors, the one that has had the longest life, extending back to the nineteenth-century work of John E. Cairne, is the "ability theory," which considers abilities to be normally distributed (that is, to have a Gaussian statistical distribution), as is the case with many physical characteristics of human beings. Many theoretical contributions clustered around the concept of ability and its dispersion, which was compatible with the skewness of the distribution.[19] Unfortunately, they appeared unsatisfactory to twentieth-century empirical testing since data were showing that specific asymmetry of a log-normal distribution. A piecemeal theoretical literature developed over time, aimed at elucidating the puzzle of personal distribution, but apparently, no fully consistent theory was ever achieved, at least at an aggregate level.[20] The task may be too demanding, as Champernowne, one of the most relevant scholars in the field of stochastic income distribution, admitted.[21] Too many forces that cause or limit inequality are at work, making any theoretical model either unrealistically simplified or hopelessly complicated. These forces – moving from social norms to institutions – pertain specifically to society and politics. Fiscal policies, for example, a quintessential political issue, have strong consequences on inequality, whether they have a redistributive bias or not.

As Nobel laureate Jan Tinbergen noticed more than fifty years ago, the statistical *description* of income distribution was much more advanced than its economic *interpretation*.[22] Almost fifty years later, Atkinson and Bourguignon again insisted that "no unified theory of income distribution actually exists. Rather than a unified theory, the literature thus offers a series of building blocks with which distribution issues are to be studied."[23] Today the situation is not substantially different, notwithstanding a flourishing new body of research. Some "building blocks" – such as skill-biased technical progress, human capital formation, and wealth accumulation – are recognized as among the main mechanisms operating on economic inequality, but a comprehensive theory is still lacking.[24]

HAD SIMON KUZNETS ANY RESPONSIBILITY FOR THE LONG SLEEP OF THEORY?

The answer might be yes, despite his intentions. An immigrant to the United States from Russia, Simon Kuznets (1901–85) was an economist and a statistician. He taught at various prestigious American universities, including Harvard, and worked at length for the National Bureau of Economic Research. He was a pioneer of historical series of national accounting along the Keynesian framework. He received the Nobel Prize in 1971 for his work on economic growth. In a famous 1955 article, "Economic Growth and Income Inequality," Kuznets looked at market income data for the United States, England, and Germany from the late nineteenth century to post-Second World War.[25] The sample was small but, as Kuznets said, was "at least a starting point for some inferences concerning long-term changes in the presently developed countries."[26]

Two relevant differences from Pareto's work were immediately visible: the use of market data instead of fiscal data, and the subject of the survey, which in the case of Pareto was the individual while in the case of Kuznets was the family-expenditure unit. Kuznets's research question was whether inequality in the distribution of income increases or decreases in the course of a country's economic growth. He developed some conjectures about the relationship between income distribution and the development of a country. "One might assume a long swing in inequality characterizing the secular income structure: widening in the early phases of economic growth when the transition from the pre-industrial to the industrial civilization was most rapid; becoming stabilized for a while; and narrowing in the later phases."[27]

Although Kuznets presented his analysis as highly tentative, he had apparently detected a correlation between the degree of economic development of a country and its domestic inequality. According to this analysis, underdeveloped economies possess low degrees of inequality. During the process of economic development – that is, as the society as a whole becomes richer – inequality initially rises, but eventually it reaches a plateau and starts to decrease while economic development proceeds.

Kuznets's hypothesis relied on a classic dualism between sectors: average income in the traditional (agricultural) sector is lower than in the modern (industrial) one, and overall differences persist even when the process of migration from the traditional sector to the advanced one has ended, owing to the diversification of jobs in the more advanced sector. As development continues, however, inequality goes down, thanks to redistributive institutions and policies. It is in advanced societies that the government starts taking a more active role in redistribution, in parallel with the progress of industrialization and unionization. Development is supposed to increase redistribution because it transforms a dispersed agrarian workforce into a more concentrated and organized industrial workforce, which thus acquires greater political awareness and power.

Plotting an inequality index against per capita GDP would show a curve resembling an inverted U, something like this: ∩, indicating an increase in inequality during the early stages of economic development and a decrease later. Notably, although today everybody refers to the Kuznets inverted-U curve, in his article Kuznets did not draw or mention any such curve, limiting himself to describing his hypothesis. More important, in the last part of his 1955 article Kuznets devoted one paragraph to the differences between developed and underdeveloped countries, arguing that "the secular income structure is somewhat more unequal in underdeveloped countries than in the more advanced [ones]."[28]

Interestingly, this idea had already been advanced in 1895 by the German social economist Gustav von Schmoller.[29] It is worthwhile recalling it because it shows that the so-called inverted-U hypothesis is more the result of a profound knowledge of economic history than of formal mathematical elaboration.

Finally, it should be noted that whereas Kuznets limited his model to describing the evolution of domestic inequality in a country undergoing development, many researchers today use it to compare countries in different stages of development at a specific moment in time, positioning them either on the rising part of the curve, or on the plateau, or on the descending part, according to the countries' relative level of development and inequality. In other words, if Kuznets was interested in describing the evolution of inequality in one country across time (and never drew the inverted-U curve that would bear his name forever), later investigators have often used the Kuznets inverted U to describe inequality in many different countries at a specific moment in time.

Kuznets's (and Schmoller's) hypothesis gave rise to a large body of theoretical and empirical research, including the official models used by organizations such as the World Bank. Its applications have extended well beyond anything envisioned by Kuznets himself, who was very cautious in presenting his findings and who warned repeatedly that he was building on very little actual evidence, and was thus engaged in little more than pure guesswork. In Kuznets's words, "In concluding this paper ... I am acutely conscious of the meagerness of reliable information presented. The paper is perhaps 5% empirical information and 95% speculation, some of it possibly tainted by wishful thinking."[30]

Kuznets's 1955 article was nonetheless interpreted by other researchers as providing a sort of law, replicable from country to country. In a sense, then, Kuznets contributed to the long sleep of inequality theory, as the general interpretation of his insight pointed at relieving possible worries about the future trend in inequality as a country progressed in its development. In fact, the inverted-U hypothesis received reasonably strong validation – though only until the 1970s, when better data and improved data-mining techniques put it in question. Today, the Kuznets inverted U can no longer be invoked – at least in the Western world – as a theory about inequality. Kuznets's analysis about the relationship between intersectoral shifts and inequality, however, remains important to understanding the process of economic growth.

After Kuznets's inverted U, as after Pareto's α, inequality researchers returned to focusing primarily on data collection and conceptual definitions, and on clarifying measures. A widely shared opinion sees this prioritization of data treatment as something noxious to the linkage between theory and empirical studies, which is looser here than in other areas of economics. On the contrary, a theory of income distribution is vital for both social science and policymaking.

Ironically, both Pareto and Kuznets may be said to share some responsibility for the continuing lack of a full theory of personal income distribution, though this can be done only at the price of some simplification. Whereas Pareto claimed to have found a historical "law" with predictive qualities, Kuznets was particularly aware of the tentativeness of his analysis and did not claim that his conclusions were a historical necessity. More modestly, he focused on intersectoral shifts and how they affect income distribution. And yet their analyses can be considered somehow to convey the same message: either inequality was a quasi-unchangeable constant (Pareto) or its fate was to disappear in the course of modernization (Kuznets). Neither view was correct. Yet these two individuals, who could not be more different in terms of temperament, vision of society, and historical context in which they worked, contributed similarly to keep the research on income distribution in economics somewhat dormant, because both shared the intellectual blind spot of approaching inequality as if it were not a political problem.

MORE ON THE LONG NEGLECT OF THEORY: WELFARE ECONOMICS, AGAIN

The neoclassical theory of distribution advanced during the first half of the twentieth century showed a substantial rejection of any normative element with the (nondeliberate) help of statistics, which focused on elaborating an "objective" index.

Inequality, however, inevitably refers to value judgments, which economics tends to handle poorly. Thus the measure of inequality should go beyond the appraisal of a distribution based on objective indices and should consider a normative approach so as to acquire awareness of what a society desires for its own members. This is something that Hugh Dalton had addressed already in the 1920s when, though not fully explicitly, he connected statistics to social welfare concerns, as we discussed in chapter 2. Dalton stressed the importance of the effects of income distribution on the total amount of social welfare more than the effects of income distribution as such. Pigou's (and Dalton's, too) transfer principle just aimed at this target.[31] Thus it was Dalton who effectively connected the descriptive with the normative aspect of measurement, stressing the important role of value judgments when measuring inequality.[32]

However, Dalton's contribution was substantially neglected for fifty years until Atkinson in 1970 reanimated the normative issue with his important advance, which would become the basis for measuring inequality in a social welfare context. What did Atkinson do in 1970? He converted welfare functions into inequality measures and vice versa, presenting the welfare-economic implications of Lorenz curve comparisons and elaborating a normative index.[33]

Atkinson proved that, under certain assumptions, the ranking of distributions according to the Lorenz curve criterion (that is, the relative position of the curves with respect to the 45-degree line together with their noncrossing, indicating greater or lesser inequality in the distribution) is identical to the ranking implied by a social welfare function satisfying some minimal assumptions.[34] Thus one distribution of income is welfare-superior to another (with the same mean) if and only if it Lorenz-dominates (that is, the welfare-superior curve is closer to the 45-degree line and the two distributions do not cross). The Lorenz curve, which was originally just a visual representation of data, an objective measure of inequality, reappeared surprisingly as a protagonist, thanks to Atkinson, and became a starting point for theory. At the end of the 1970s the Lorenz ordering found a multitude of applications in theoretical statistics, and today the Lorenz curve is still the basis of many applications in public finance and studies of growth and poverty.

In this process of merging inequality and welfare, Atkinson elaborated an index – one obeying the three main properties of a good index: independence on the mean of the distribution, symmetry, and transfer sensitivity – able to provide a normative basis for the measurement of income inequality.

This index, like the Gini index, lies between zero (complete equality) and 1 (complete inequality).[35] However, the meaning is different: in Atkinson's index, a value of 0.30 means that "if incomes were equally distributed then we should need only 70% of the present national income to achieve the same level of social welfare."[36] In simpler terms, the index gives us the welfare loss (30 per cent in the above example) of current inequality. Moreover, since this index varies according to a parameter ϵ – which indicates the society's aversion to inequality[37] – it goes well beyond a simple measurement. When ϵ equals zero, there is complete indifference toward inequality, while a positive and increasing value of ϵ up to infinity means an increasingly higher propensity to redistribution so as to favor individuals in the bottom part. Thus, "not only does this close correspondence serve the purpose of constructing new measures of inequality, but it also helps in uncovering the implicit value judgments in inequality indicators that are used without specifying any welfare assumption."[38]

WHAT ELSE? STATISTICAL TOOLS FOR AN AUGMENTED VISION OF INEQUALITY

Distributive justice – with a focus primarily on defining what societies want – was thoroughly studied in the second half of the twentieth century. Within that vivid debate, (in)equality was thrown into the stormy waters of modern moral philosophy and social choice theory, emerging once more as a hardly measurable concept.

However, that debate also challenged the measurement realm of inequality, shifting the interest toward a multidimensional approach. The need to consider, within the concept of inequality, aspects that are external to the pure economic dominion, yet without losing any formal rigor in measurement, became in the second half of the twentieth century a blossoming area of research in both statistics and mathematics applied to social sciences.

This research was undoubtedly inspired by Sen's capability approach,[39] according to which society should consider what people are able to be and to do, and should be concerned about the quality of life well beyond utility or income. In Sen's approach, the two relevant categories are functionings (good health, literacy, and so on) and capabilities. Functionings are "beings and doings," that is, what we are and what we do, whereas capabilities are "the opportunities to achieve functionings."[40] Capabilities can thus be considered an indicator of freedom. Unfortunately, the capability approach has remained almost entirely theoretical because both the weighting structure and the substitutability of the functionings hide implicit value judgments, which are still – and perhaps will always be – an unsolved aspect in terms of actual measurement.

Multidimensional measures of inequality within a normative approach have been the subject of extensive recent research.[41] As a general strategy, the bifurcation either stays within considering each dimension in its singularity or conflates multidimensionality into one indicator: either to derive multiple indices that can be applied directly to the vectors of various attributes or to specify a composite index and then compute a univariate inequality index. Technical and nontechnical advantages and drawbacks are present with both choices.

Researchers have elaborated theoretically refined and empirically challenging measures that have not yet emerged from the specialists' sphere to reach a wider audience. The unique multidimensional index whose application has extended beyond that of a small group of specialists and is now being used worldwide for socioeconomic evaluations is the Human Development Index (HDI), which has the relevant merit of having raised awareness of the connection of politics to the inequality issue. The multidimensionality of this index resides in its considering income together with life expectancy and educational achievement, and then averaging over these three values.[42] Not surprisingly, Sen has described it as a "vulgar" measure, with almost the same level of crudeness as GNP.[43] Much remains to be done, therefore, to build a multidimensional and statistically strong measure.

At the end of the day, the question of why there is no theory of inequality can be considered answered – or it can be rejected as the wrong question. In fact, we may consider that the quasi-absence of the personal distribution concept in economics until roughly a century ago, combined with a mere computational effort, may have left no room or energy for a widespread inquiry into the causes of inequality, giving an objective explanation to the puzzle. Or we may consider that the search for an explanation of the causes of inequality risks becoming pointless since inequality is solely a lack of equality, and agreement on both the concept of equality and what degree of equality is wanted seems, at least presently, out of reach. Thus societies must determine what degree of fairness and ethics is wanted and always renegotiate a difficult balance.

FOUR

Inequality and Globalization

> There is currently no such thing as global equality of opportunity: a lot of our income depends on the accident of birth.
>
> Branko Milanovic, *Global Inequality*

Huge international migratory flows are a distinct feature of the last thirty to fifty years, depending on the countries of destination. The flow of migrants toward Europe began well before the collapse of Syria and Libya, one result of the abysmal differences between many poor non-European regions and Europe.[1] In particular, economic migration from sub-Saharan Africa continues stronger than ever, as migrants seek to escape poverty and inequality.[2] They don't see a future at home, and they feel they have nothing to lose: "I'd rather die than go back to my country," a young Somali man ready to cross at the port of Misrata, Libya, explained to a *Le Monde* reporter. "Going back to Somalia, to that sense of insecurity, to that poverty, is inconceivable to me. I would try to leave for Europe as soon as I was sent back. I'd rather die than give up."[3]

As data on global migrations before and after the onset of the global economic crisis in 2008 confirm, international economic inequality is crucial to understanding migratory flows. Whereas in the years 2000–10 the number of migrants grew at a rate of approximately 4.6 million annually (in absolute terms, from approximately 174 million to 220 million), in the current decade, when advanced economies have experienced a dramatic slowdown, the number of migrants has grown at the lower rate of approximately 3.6 million annually.[4] Prospective migrants know that economic opportunities are shrinking even in advanced economies, and some decide not to leave or to postpone leaving.

A BIRD'S-EYE VIEW OF GLOBALIZATION

Migrations typically occur during globalizing waves, though national policies often try to restrain them. As the historians Jürgen Osterhammel and Niels Petersson remind us, globalizing processes have always been characterized by important migratory movements. The spread of a religious *ecumene* – roughly, a transnational community – under Islam in the eighth century and of the Mongol Empire in the thirteen century are early instances of globalizing processes, although both eventually reversed.[5] Migrations are powerful globalizing mechanisms as they spread customs, beliefs, languages, traditions, commercial and financial networks, techniques, flora and fauna, and less visible yet important new elements such as genes and bacteria.[6] But migrations are in turn the product of globalizing dynamics originating in other spheres, such as political and territorial aggregation, military conquests, and international trade and financial globalization.

The economic history of the last two centuries is, in this sense, paradigmatic, for the global economy in the nineteenth century became increasingly interconnected – world trade, for example, increased much more than global production – and migratory flows increased accordingly. Between 1850 and 1914, approximately 65 million people left their countries for good, mainly as a consequence of systemic economic changes.[7] Finally, the current Mediterranean migration underscores that migrations are a fundamental factor directly affecting and affected by inequality dynamics at the global level. People's ability to migrate is not only an unmistakable sign that globalizing forces are at work; it is also one of the principal mechanisms for individuals to raise their standard of living and increase their position in the global income distribution.

The example of migrations shows that the phenomenon of globalization is complex and multifaceted, intimately connected to the imbalances of inequality. Globalization has a cultural dimension, for it is associated both with the spread of hegemonic cultures globally and with the somewhat opposite phenomenon of cultural hybridization. Also, it affects political dynamics at the national, regional, and global level. Nation-states are embedded in economic and political processes that are increasingly global, implying a reassessment of national sovereignty and often triggering processes of fragmentation and territorial and political reconfiguration in the form of separatist movements or, at the opposite pole, macroregional agglomeration. At the global level, these dynamics affect the long-term balance of power among global macroregions. Globalization, in sum, integrates a number of different processes within a single comprehensive framework.[8]

Researchers have often approached globalization as a process that unfolds in the very long run. Kocka and Osterhammel and Petersson, as we have seen, cite the spread of Islam in the eighth century and of the Mongol Empire in the thirteenth century as instances of globalization, but also notice that those instances never reached the tipping point of irreversibility, and sooner or later ceased. Other historians have focused instead on the formation of colonial empires at the beginning of the sixteenth century as the start of an irreversible process of global economic integration. Immanuel Wallerstein, for example, described the European economy in the sixteenth century as the nucleus of a European "world economic system" that in time would aggregate other areas of the globe as peripheries to that core.[9] Wallerstein's analysis was just one of a number of seminal studies on the globalization of economic processes from the fifteenth century on, such as those by the French historian Fernand Braudel and the sociologists Giovanni Arrighi and Beverly Silver.[10]

Those processes had not been neglected by an earlier, very prominent commentator: in the first volume of *Das Kapital*, Karl Marx wrote that "the discovery of gold and silver in America, the extirpation, enslavement and entombment in mines of the indigenous population of that continent, the beginnings of the conquest and plunder of India, and the conversion of Africa into a preserve for the commercial hunting of blackskins, are all things which characterize the dawn of the era of capitalist production." On the heels of those "idyllic proceedings," he concluded, trod "the commercial war of the European nations, which has the globe as its battlefield."[11] Many will consider Marx a biased observer, yet he was accurately depicting the relationship between globalization and inequality.

Other historians have studied globalization, and in particular economic globalization, as a distinctively modern phenomenon. The Harvard economic historian Jeffrey G. Williamson places the "first global century" in the nineteenth century, between 1820 and 1913: "In spite of all the attention that the Age of Discovery and the Age of Commerce get from historians, the descriptive phrase 'global economy' only applied to a tiny share of world economic activity before the nineteenth century."[12] In this sense, globalization refers mainly to deeper international economic integration, and this is the dimension we will privilege in the rest of this chapter.

During the so-called first and second waves of globalization (ca. 1870–1914 and 1950–mid-1970s, respectively), between-country inequality increased, while domestic inequality, at least for those countries that underwent an industrial revolution, seemed to follow Kuznets's hypothesis of an inverted-U trajectory: at first inequality increased, and in later stages of economic growth it decreased.

These downward within-country inequality trends have in past decades undergone a staggering U-turn. Today the social compact that after the Second World War kept together economic expansion and social justice in many countries is quickly eroding. This erosion has caused increasing tensions, discontent, and social anomie, which are changing the nature of many of the world's democracies. This condition is obviously affected by global phenomena and transformations. Kuznets's inverted-U curve apparently no longer applies, and whereas between-country inequality has begun to decrease, within-country inequality is again on the rise. As François Bourguignon has recently argued, "The central question is whether the increase in inequality observed in the United States, in some European countries, and in some emerging countries may be considered the consequence of a globalizing process, which, at the same time, has drastically reduced income differences between developed and developing countries."[13] In other words, how can we interpret the interplay between globalization and within- and between-country inequality? This chapter discusses some of the literature that can help us answer this question.

Another question, however, must be also discussed, namely,

the consequences of these changes in the dynamics of inequality for national societies. Increasing inequality within specific countries directly affects those countries' social fabric and democratic institutions. We discuss this dimension in chapter 5, devoted to inequality and democracy.

DIFFERENT CONCEPTS OF BETWEEN-COUNTRY INEQUALITY

Between-country inequality can be observed from a number of different perspectives. First, we can study the inequality resulting from differences in the per capita gross domestic product (GDP) of different countries. Depending on whether the countries are weighted by their population or not, as discussed in the appendix, this inequality is referred to as "world" and "international" inequality respectively. Second, we can study the inequality resulting from income differences among all the citizens of the world as if they all belonged to one single country, which we call "global" inequality. Global inequality thus combines the measure of population-weighted inequality across nations with the measure of the inequality existing within each country.

Whereas the concept of global inequality will eventually supplant the concept of population-weighted international inequality as a more accurate measure of basically the same phenomenon (that is, the level of inequality in the world), unweighted international inequality – that is, the inequality among countries in the world, as if every country, from the highly populated to the barely inhabited, counted the same – enjoys a certain consideration among students of inequality. One of them, for example, suggests that for purposes of policymaking, treating countries as if all counted the same makes sense, because it allows investigators to observe what works and why, irrespective of a country's size.[14] The size of a country, however, clearly does affect many policy decisions and the likelihood that they will be successful, for what is possible in a large country may not even be conceivable in a small one. This concept especially has recently been at the core of an important debate on whether globalization is correlated with an increase or a decrease in international inequality.

More precisely, the discussion has revolved around whether globalization has helped less developed countries catch up to more advanced countries, and thus around whether average incomes in developed and less developed countries are converging or, on the contrary, whether globalization has further increased the income gap between less developed and more developed countries. For this reason, this debate is known as the convergence debate.

INEQUALITY BETWEEN COUNTRIES: GLOBALIZATION AND THE CONVERGENCE DEBATE

Standard economic theory predicts economic convergence. Especially in a setting characterized by open trade and the free circulation of ideas, capital, commodities, and people, countries that are economically underdeveloped can tap into and adapt to their needs a huge storehouse of technological and administrative knowledge, and in this way can catch up to the most advanced economies. This notion of catching up, or convergence, was espoused by William Baumol three decades ago when he noticed that in the decades following 1870, when the first wave of globalization began gaining momentum, most market economies caught up to the leader. Moreover, the higher the productivity of a country in 1870, the slower that country's productivity grew in the next hundred years. In other words, countries that were underdeveloped in 1870 gained more ground than the economically advanced countries. This trend toward convergence included not only advanced free-market economies but also "intermediate" and planned economies; only the very poorest underdeveloped countries did not participate in the trend at all.[15]

Baumol's interest in convergence trends was initially prompted by specific US *national* preoccupations. As concerns were mounting over the slowdown in US productivity and the perceived erosion of the country's leadership position in the late 1960s and early 1970s, Baumol sought to show that convergence, especially productivity convergence, was a constant of long-term economic history. It was not that US productivity was falling below its past record, as the alarmists claimed. The explanation was simpler and much less worrisome: the US economy was performing well, but other industrial countries were stepping up productivity and approaching US levels.

Baumol's article triggered an exchange with the economists J. Bradford DeLong and Edward N. Wolff that soon put aside the specific question of the place of the United States among advanced economies to reignite an illustrious tradition of studies about the broader phenomenon of international convergence.[16] Baumol was adamant in claiming that the only pattern that counted in the convergence path was the trade-off between 1870 productivity levels and future growth: "What is striking is the apparent implication that *only one variable*, a country's 1870 GDP per work-hour, or its relation to that of the productivity leader, matters to any substantial degree." The institutional setting and the presence or absence of trade openness, high investment ratios, and industrial policies did not count much: "Whatever its behavior, that nation was apparently fated to land close to its predestined position."[17] The only exception was the poorest among the less developed countries, which had not followed a catching-up pattern and instead had increasingly lagged behind, probably because of an insurmountable gap in educational and technological levels that made it impossible to absorb advances in knowledge from more developed countries. Less developed countries were thus excluded by history from the "convergence club."

Against Baumol's bold linearity and insistence on a sort of historical predestination, economists and economic historians discovered that the historical record in fact falsified the convergence prediction, or showed convergence in periods when nobody would expect it, such as during the interwar, ultra-protectionist, and antiglobalizing years. In the late 1980s, thus, the question of income convergence met globalization studies, prompted by the collapse of the Bretton Woods system and the liberalization of financial flows, and the convergence prediction turned into the much more contentious convergence debate. In that debate lie important seeds of current work on between-country economic inequality.

The point, of course, was not really convergence among the countries that by the second half of the twentieth century were considered to be "advanced capitalist" countries. DeLong in 1988 and the World Bank economist Lant Pritchett in 1997 both noticed that Baumol's sample *guaranteed* the finding of historical convergence, as Baumol had chosen countries whose economies were actually advanced when his article was published in 1988. Baumol's sample, in other words, was biased, as Pritchett put it, because "either countries are rich now and were rich historically, in which case they all have had roughly the same growth rate (like nearly all of Europe), or countries are rich now and were poor historically (like Japan) and hence grew faster and show convergence." A study of countries that had in fact converged could only show convergence, and was "almost tautological."[18] Only an ex ante analysis of the economic trajectory of countries that back in 1870 had shown the potential to converge would have avoided this tautological result. And once one avoided Baumol's bias, the results were different. An unbiased sample of countries that in 1870s were credible candidates for convergence, DeLong noticed, had not converged.[19] Argentina, which in the late nineteenth century was relatively rich but later lagged behind, is a case in point.

But not only convergence appeared not to be a historical necessity. Pritchett remarked that once one considered both advanced and less developed countries at the end of the twentieth century and one century earlier, the relative trajectories could instead be summed up as "divergence, big time."[20] This discrepancy between convergence and globalization trends shook the foundations of a benign reading of globalization. Pritchett noticed that convergence had occurred only among European countries and other temperate regions of European settlement (called in the literature the European offshoots) plus Japan, whereas the growth rates of less developed countries had on average been slower than those of advanced countries, therefore producing divergence in relative incomes. The only positive note in this analysis is that the pattern was not the same for all less developed countries, which in the postwar period showed very different trajectories. While certain countries have indeed stagnated, others have shown remarkable growth ratios.[21]

The convergence debate sheds light on a much more varied scenario. To start with, the period of incubation of the first wave of globalization (1820–70) was characterized by convergence, although at first only among England, Belgium, and the northeastern United States. Later, during the first globalizing wave proper (1870–1914), convergence involved also other temperate regions, such as Canada, New Zealand, Australia, the US West

Coast, Chile, and Argentina. Outside this small group of countries, the first era of globalization did not produce any converging trend. The convergence club seemed instead to become larger during the deglobalizing period between the two world wars, when additional countries in Latin America, the Soviet area, Japan and its Korean empire, and parts of coastal Africa such as Ghana, the Ivory Coast, Kenya, Tanzania, Nigeria, Morocco, Algeria, and Tunisia began to close the gap that separated their economies from the advanced ones.

Finally, the postwar globalizing era marked, during the second wave (1950 to mid-1970s), the completion of the convergence process among advanced economies. During the third globalizing wave (post-1980), a number of less developed economies have accelerated, especially highly populated China and India and the Asian tigers, but many other countries in Africa, Latin America, and the former Communist bloc have lagged behind. The convergence club has thus acquired some important members, but it has also lost a number of members that were previously in it or nearly in it, such as Argentina, South Africa, the countries of Mediterranean Africa, and various countries that were part of the former Soviet Union.[22]

While scholars such as Robert Barro argue that globalization has indeed succeeded in fostering convergence, as many additional countries have joined the club of advanced economies, other authors have noticed that over the past forty years, that is, more or less during the third wave of globalization, income levels have in fact been diverging, and we are witnessing today unprecedented levels of between-country inequality.[23]

The economic historians Peter H. Lindert and Jeffrey G. Williamson, who accept this conclusion, have also noticed, however, that the dramatic widening of income gaps between nations can be dated back at least to 1600 CE, if not earlier. Although based on only partial information, especially for the most distant periods, Lindert and Williamson's conclusion is nonetheless that "the early modern 'great divergence' was true in all dimensions – globally *and* between European nations *and* within European nations."[24]

And yet what looks like an unproblematic claim opens the door to a question of the utmost importance, that is, whether globalization is actually responsible for the increasing inequality that is unfolding before our eyes. If global divergence has been, in Pritchett's terms, "big time" for at least 400 years, globalization has a much shorter history, dating back to the early nineteenth century at the most. How, Lindert and Williamson ask, could globalization (less than 200 years old) be responsible for rising world inequality (more than 400 years old)?[25]

In particular, through a complex analysis of the diverse elements that characterize national and international economic processes, Lindert and Williamson show how globalization affected different economies in very different ways. For example, during the first globalizing era, access to international markets and mass migrations affected rich, land-abundant New World countries and poor, land-scarce European countries in opposite ways: within-country inequality increased in the former and decreased in the latter. Some poor primary-product-exporting countries, which were the destination of mass migratory flows, as were other land-abundant New World countries, and which, like them, showed increasing domestic inequality, witnessed in addition the phenomenon of deindustrialization and ensuing lower long-term economic growth. As a consequence, they lagged behind rich New World countries, which instead attracted capital and entered on a path of self-sustained growth. In other words, primary-product-exporting countries experienced increasing inequality both within and between countries.[26]

The major point of Lindert and Williamson's contribution is that within-country and between-country inequality are not the outcome of globalization. The rise in inequality, and especially the rise in between-country inequality that characterizes the last two centuries, is in their opinion caused by large areas of the world remaining at the margins of the globalizing waves.[27] In his analysis of the world economy, Angus Maddison made very much the same point, underscoring how the deglobalizing period of 1914–50 saw an acceleration in the rise of between-country inequality.[28]

As far as within-country inequality is concerned, while admitting that this phenomenon is of less unequivocal interpretation, Lindert and Williamson still attribute it to an excessively low degree of openness to globalizing processes. In their discussion of China, India, Indonesia, and Russia, for example, they claim that "the rise in [within-country] inequality appears to have been based on the exclusion of much of the population from the benefits of globalization."[29]

A number of analyses that reach the same conclusions have been advanced, so much so that we can consider this reading of the relationship between globalization and inequality trends as the orthodox position. In fact, already between the late 1960s and the 1970s a number of studies had attacked protectionist policies in less developed countries in favor of trade openness and liberalization, arguing that "promoting" industry instead of "protecting" it was the correct trade policy for newly industrializing countries. These studies, in other words, disregarding the structural difference between industrially advanced and less developed countries, argued that protectionist barriers should be eliminated in favor of policies aimed at enhancing the efficiency and international competitiveness of the industrial sector.[30] Subsequent studies have often shown, if not a causal relationship, at least a correlation between increasing globalization and decreasing inequality. In a much cited issue of the *Oxford Review of Economic Policy*, Andrea Boltho and Gianni Toniolo described a rise in the Gini coefficient of population-weighted between-country inequality during the 1940s, followed by a plateau in the subsequent three decades, and finally an important fall after 1980 (remember that the higher the Gini coefficient, the higher is inequality).[31] Boltho and Toniolo introduced a new and important element in the analysis of world inequality. The turning point of 1980, after which between-country world inequality decreased to pre-1950 levels, was caused by an acceleration in the rate of growth of the two most populous countries in the world, India and China.[32] These two countries have a crucial influence on trends of world and global inequality.

One institution that has more consistently highlighted the beneficial effects of globalization on inequality has been the World Bank. The World Bank's analysis of inequality has often appeared to be a by-product of its focus on economic growth. Still, the correlation between globalization and decreasing inequality has been made consistently explicit. The flagship annual World Bank publication, the *World Development Report*, has often insisted on this relationship. Specifically, according to the 1987 and 1994 reports, the average GDP per capita of strongly outward-oriented and moderately outward-oriented countries grew, in the 1963–73 period, by 6.9 and 4.9 per cent, respectively. After a pronounced slowing during the turbulent decade of the 1970s and early 1980s (to 5.9 and 1.6 per cent, respectively), those figures recuperated in the subsequent globalizing period (to 6.4 and 2.3 per cent, respectively). Inward-oriented countries, by contrast, showed a much worse record: 4.0 and 1.6 per cent for the moderately and strongly protectionist countries, respectively, during the 1963–73 period; 1.7 and –0.1 per cent, respectively, during the 1970s; and –0.2 and –0.4 per cent during the third globalizing wave.[33]

Two conclusions could be drawn from these data. First, while outward-oriented countries consistently benefited from participating in the world economy, inward-oriented economies declined and then went into a nosedive. Second, the more open an economy is, the higher its growth rate appears to be.

Obviously, this directly affects inequality trends, if not at the domestic level, undoubtedly at the international level. According to a widely circulated 2002 World Bank report, "Globalization generally reduces poverty because more integrated economies tend to grow faster and this growth is usually widely diffused." As the report recognized, many countries, totaling about 2 billion people, had remained untouched by the globalizing process and so had fallen behind. Unfavorable geography, weak institutions, or endemic civil war were among the main causes for these countries' increasing marginalization. Countries that instead adopted outward-oriented policies highly benefited from them. Within-country inequality was not necessarily affected, and when it was, only with much variation among countries. During the 1990s, however, new globalizing developing countries grew at an average 5 per cent per year, against an average 2 per cent of advanced countries. As the report pointed out, "Between countries, globalization is now mostly reducing inequality."[34]

Orthodoxy does not mean unanimity, however, and so some researchers have questioned this benign reading of globalization. Branko Milanovic, at the time an economist at the World Bank, criticized this mainstream view of globalization as at best "naïve," at worst "self-interested," and at any rate misleadingly "Polyannaish." As he writes, "It is only a slight caricaturization of this naïve view to state that its proponents regard globalization as a *deus ex machina* for many of the problems such as poverty, illiteracy or inequality that beset the developing world."[35] Specifically, Milanovic criticizes the historical analysis as depicted by scholars such as Lindert and Williamson. First, the Atlantic economy that, according to Lindert and Williamson, has been at the core of the globalization process has not shown, as they claim, any unquestionable convergence trend. The historical evidence, in Milanovic's view, is far from conclusive, and depending on which statistics one adopts, one could argue that even among core countries globalization was accompanied by increasing divergence. Second, in the nineteenth century many less developed countries were forced to participate in the process of globalization by way of gunboat diplomacy and colonialism. As Milanovic writes, "Globalization was not merely *accompanied* by the worst excesses of colonialism; colonialism was not an accident. On the contrary, globalization *was* colonialism because it is through being colonies that most of the non-European countries were brought to the global world." Remarkably, in the analysis of Lindert and Williamson never once are the words "colonialism," "colony," "slavery," or "colonization" mentioned.[36] And yet it was during the nineteenth century that the largest among the future third world countries were inserted into the global economy led by the core Atlantic economies. During this century, we can observe both an absolute and a relative decline of less developed countries compared to advanced economies. This does not necessarily mean, as many theorists of dependency claim, that the economic growth of the West was rooted in imperial rule and colonialism, but it certainly shows that the economic stagnation and impoverishment of the global south was correlated to colonial exploitation.[37]

Milanovic has also reassessed the analysis of the postwar globalizing waves, and again, he has not found evidence of correlation (let alone causation) between globalization and economic growth. From calculations based on various different sources, he notes that during the second wave, which he dates to 1960–78,

GDP per capita growth rates were much higher than in the subsequent period, 1978–98, which was characterized by increasing trade openness and the shrinking of the welfare state and safety nets in many countries. If in the first period Africa's GDP per capita (weighted by the population) grew by 1.5 per cent per year, Asia's by 4.0, Latin America's by 2.8, Eastern Europe's and the former Soviet Union states' by 5.1, Western Europe's and its offshoots' by 2.9, and the world's, on average, by 2.7 per cent per year, in the second period Africa's GDP per capita grew by a miserable 0.1 per cent per year, Asia's by 3.6, Latin America's by 0.8, Eastern Europe's and the former Soviet Union states' by –1.1, Western Europe's and its offshoots' by 1.6, and the world's, on average, by 1.4 per cent per year. Especially in the case of Asia, the rate's fall was limited owing to the large weight that China's and India's growth received because of their large populations. The unweighted Asian growth rate would otherwise have plummeted from 6.3 per cent per year in 1960–78 to 0.9 per cent per year in 1978–98.[38]

These data prompt us to reflect on how these very large countries and their huge populations affect the analysis and interpretation of inequality at the world level. Whereas economists today agree that in the last two centuries, incomes across the world have dramatically diverged, they still identify profound differences in the role, if any, that globalization has had on this divergence. In the preceding paragraph, the analysis of the growth rates of GDP per capita in the second and third globalizing waves, first referring to population-weighted data and then, with a focus on Asia, to unweighted data, shows how results can dramatically change and lead to opposite conclusions. Later in the chapter we broaden the discussion to global inequality (that is, a combination of between-country and within-country inequality) and see how it can help us better understand inequality trends, with a special focus on the third globalizing wave. First, however, we are interested in what happened to within-country inequality in the earlier globalization periods.

WITHIN-COUNTRY INEQUALITY DURING THE FIRST AND SECOND GLOBALIZATION WAVES

The first globalization wave corresponded to the first age of industrialization. Until then, human societies had been agrarian economies and operated according to a Malthusian logic: incomes, in other words, would move up and down pro-cyclically with mortality rates and wars. Inequality rates, in pre-industrial economies, could not be particularly high. Obviously, pharaohs, emperors, medieval princes, and members of the elite could be (and often were) staggeringly rich, but the average income of the large mass of the population was usually not significantly above subsistence level. This can be easily grasped intuitively, but we can also rely on some more articulated analyses. Milanovic, Lindert, and Williamson, after their polemics over convergence, joined forces to document inequality levels in the pre-industrial world.[39] They found that in many societies the average income was only approximately twice the subsistence income. In the Roman Empire in 14 CE, for example, the mean income was 2.1 times the subsistence minimum; in Byzantium in the year 1000 CE, the mean income was 1.8 times the subsistence minimum; in England and Wales in 1290 CE it was 2.1 times the subsistence minimum, and so on. Only in eighteenth-century Holland, the metropolis of a powerful commercial empire, did the mean income escape this low value: it was 6.8 times the subsistence minimum, almost the same as in England and Wales in 1801 CE (6.7).[40]

Based on these data, Milanovic, Lindert, and Williamson were able to build what they called an "inequality possibility frontier" and an "inequality extraction ratio." The former refers to the maximum possible inequality attainable in a society. To recall, in principle the Gini coefficient can reach a value of 1 (or 100, depending on the scale we use) when the entire population does not receive any income and one individual receives the entire income. This is the theoretical value of extreme inequality, although in actuality it is impossible: those who did not receive any income would die and the society would quickly collapse and disappear. In fact, all individuals usually receive at least what is needed to survive, which is a subsistence income. What remains after the subsistence income has been distributed to all individuals in a population is what elites can actually take for themselves. This quantity, and the corresponding Gini coefficient, is the "inequality possibility frontier." Clearly, the closer the mean income is to the subsistence minimum, the less surplus is available for the elites to seize, and hence the maximum possible inequality will be relatively low. The higher the mean income is in comparison to the subsistence minimum, the higher will be the surplus that elites can seize, and thus the higher the Gini coefficient can be. The inequality possibility frontier is a very valuable concept as it disregards the extreme cases that arise in the theory of the Gini index and provides a framework with which to gauge the actual inequality coefficient of a society with regard not to a theoretical 1 (or 100) but to the maximum possible inequality that allows a society to survive. This way of calculating the Gini coefficient is expressed by the following equation:

$$G^* (\mu) = (\alpha - 1)/\alpha,$$

where G^* denotes the maximum feasible Gini coefficient for a given level of overall mean income (μ), and α (which is not Pareto's

α, discussed in chapter 3) is the multiple of the subsistence minimum income. Clearly, if a society has resources only adequate for all its members to receive a subsistence minimum, inequality will be impossible. In terms of the equation, $\alpha = 1$ and $G^* = 0$. As we have seen from the historical examples of the Roman Empire, Byzantium, Holland, England, and Wales, however, the mean income is virtually always a multiple of the subsistence minimum, though often not a huge multiple. With $\alpha > 1$, a surplus becomes available, elites may be able to seize it (how much of it is a matter of their political and coercive power, ability, and historical accident), and inequality arises. Figure 4.1 shows the maximum feasible Gini coefficient in relation to a society's mean income, expressed as a multiple of the subsistence minimum.

The ratio between the actual inequality and the maximum possible inequality is the "inequality extraction ratio," that is, how much of the feasible maximum inequality the elites are actually able to extract from society. On average, Milanovic, Lindert, and Williamson found that pre-industrial elites were able to extract three quarters of the maximum feasible inequality from their societies.[41]

Another important characteristic of inequality in the pre-industrial era is that historically, it moved up and down very irregularly, without showing any specific pattern. As Milanovic puts it, "Before the Industrial Revolution, when mean income was stagnant, there was no relationship between mean income level and the level of inequality. Wages and inequality were driven up or down by idiosyncratic events such as epidemics or other catastrophic events, new discoveries (of the Americas or of new trade routes between Europe and Asia), invasions, and wars." The upper boundary of the Gini index was, at the height of the Roman Empire in 150 CE, more than 40 points; it was at 20–25

Figure 4.1. The inequality possibility frontier according to Milanovic, Lindert, and Williamson

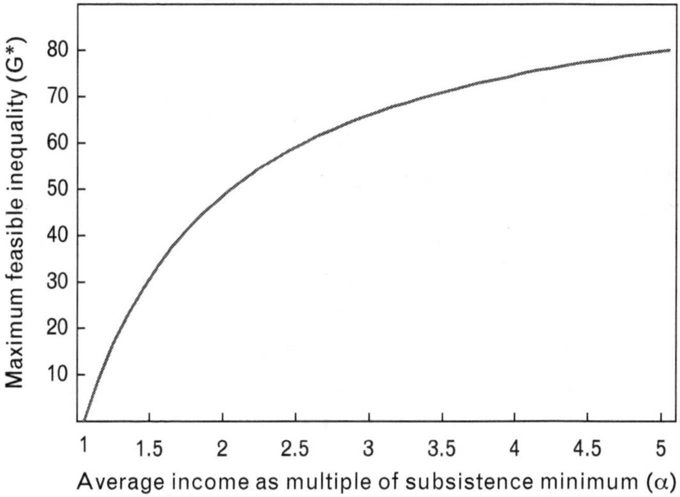

Source: Branko Milanovic, Peter H. Lindert, and Jeffrey G. Williamson, "Pre-Industrial Inequality," *Economic Journal* 121, no. 551 (2011), figure 1, p. 258.

points in the fourth and fifth centuries and at 15 points in 700 CE. Gini coefficients (related, in this case, to wealth, not income) in northwestern Italy spanned between 52 and 85 from the early fourteenth century to the late eighteenth century, while in the Low Countries in 1400–1850 CE. they spanned between a low of 35 and a high of 56. In sum, inequality moved in "undulating waves" around a stable average income level.[42]

With the Industrial Revolution and the onset of a process of self-sustaining economic growth and urbanization, first in England and then in a number of other European countries and some other European offshoots, average incomes began to grow, and, following Kuznets, within-country inequality in industrializing countries increased for approximately a century, reached a plateau at the turn of the twentieth century or somewhat later, and began to decrease thereafter until the end of the second globalizing phase was reached, more or less in the late 1970s. This inverted-U trajectory corresponded to the transition from agriculture to industry. The essential point of Kuznets's analysis, as one scholar lucidly put it, was thus that "the key determinant of economic inequality is the structural composition of the economy itself" (we will elaborate on this structural dimension later, in the section on global inequality).[43]

Of course, countries were not fully synchronized in their intersectoral transition, and, depending on the specific country, the Kuznets curve lasted a shorter or longer time, began earlier or later, was more or less steep, and lasted longer between its peak and its trough. Scholars have reconstructed in detail the Kuznets inverted-U curve for a number of countries, and we summarize their results in table 4.1.

The downward trend of the Kuznets curve was due to a number of factors, some positive and some negative, such as the closing gap between rural and urban wages; the reduction in return on capital; destruction of capital, higher taxation, and inflation caused by the two world wars; and major political shifts in favor of inclusive and redistributive policies. Thomas Piketty in particular has recently highlighted the correlation between wars and decreasing inequality, showing how wars inverted, at least temporarily, the basic imbalance between the rate of return on financial wealth and the growth rate of the economy. If the former is usually higher than the latter, and thus inequality rises, the destruction of war, higher taxation to finance war production, inflation, and specific government policies hold capital gains in check, causing inequality to decrease. Piketty has been as much

Table 4.1. Kuznets inverted U's: years and Gini coefficients

COUNTRY	INITIAL POINT		PEAK		FINAL TROUGH	
	YEAR	GINI	YEAR	GINI	YEAR	GINI
United States	1774	45	1933	50	1979	35
United Kingdom	1688	45	1867	58	1962	28
Spain	1850	38	1953	54	1985	31
Italy[a]	n.a.	n.a.	1860	51	1983	30
Netherlands	1561	55	1732	62	1982	28
Brazil	1850	39	1920–90	55–64	2012	49
Chile I	1850	52	1873	59	1903	47
Chile II[b]	1903	47	1939	62	1970	51
Japan	1895	42	1937	55	1962	35

Source: Data from Branko Milanovic, *Global Inequality: A New Approach for the Age of Globalization* (Belknap Press of Harvard University Press, 2016), pp. 70–91, reporting data from studies by Branko Milanovic, Peter H. Lindert, and Jeffrey G. Williamson; Daniel B. Radner and John C. Hinrichs; Eugene Smolensky and Robert Plotnick; Selma Goldsmith, George Jaszi, Hyman Kaitz, and Maurice Liebenberg; Jonathan Cribb; Angus Maddison; Leandro Prados de la Escosura; Andrea Brandolini and Giovanni Vecchi; Lee Soltow and Jan Luiten van Zanden; Luiz Bértola, Cecilia Castelnovo, Javier Rodríguez, and Henry Willebald; Rodrìguez Weber; and Ryoshin Minami.

a. For Italy, data availability starts at the time of political unification, in 1861, and follows a continuous downward trend; therefore, no initial point data are available (n.a.).

b. Chile is decomposed into Chile I and Chile II because in the period that for other countries corresponded to the evolution of one classic Kuznets inverted-U curve, Chile experienced *two* Kuznets inverted-U curves. In fact, Chile offers an early example of what Milanovic calls Kuznets "waves" and Pedro Conceição and James Galbraith refer to as the "augmented Kuznets hypothesis." See Pedro Conceição and James K. Galbraith, "Toward a New Kuznets Hypothesis: Theory and Evidence on Growth and Inequality," in *Inequality and Industrial Change: A Global View,* edited by James K. Galbraith and Maureen Berner (Cambridge University Press, 2001), pp. 139–60.

praised as criticized, but this short history is not the place to open the Pandora's box of this vast and ever-growing debate. It is worth mentioning, however, the most creative neologism attributed to Piketty's work – "gattopardo economics."[44] The endnote offers references for the reader interested in the debate kindled by Piketty's work.[45] Others, in particular those engaged in Marxist-flavored analyses, also have underscored the relationship between wars and inequality while insisting that the greater role was played by an earlier unsustainable domestic inequality, which triggered external aggression.[46]

Finally, a long period after the Second World War was characterized by the Cold War, which made welfare state policies particularly important in the ideological battle against the communist camp. The Cold War ended only at the end of the 1980s with the reopening of the borders between Hungary and Western Europe (followed by the opening of the borders between all other countries in the Soviet sphere), the fall of the Berlin Wall, and the dissolution of the Soviet Union. Those events deeply changed the global context. In particular, the spread of the capitalist system to (almost) the entire world, communist China included, became a crucial turning point in world history. Francis Fukuyama, then deputy director of the US State Department's policy planning staff, famously wrote that the "unabashed victory of economic and political liberalism" marked nothing less than "the end of history as such: that is, the end point of mankind's ideological evolution and the universalization of Western liberal democracy as the final form of human government."[47]

History in fact has not ended, but that passage was nonetheless crucial, marking the beginning of a more unfettered and deeper wave of globalization.

GLOBAL INEQUALITY

If we try to summarize what happened to inequality from the Industrial Revolution to approximately 1980, that is, the eve of the third globalizing wave, we can say that individual countries that underwent a process of industrialization also saw their economy go through a Kuznets curve. At the same time, between-country inequality was characterized by increasing divergence. During the nineteenth century, then, inequality grew both within and between countries, and those trends continued for most of the twentieth century. While inequality among countries, however, continued unaltered, industrial countries eventually saw their domestic inequality reach a plateau and then decrease. This is the phenomenon referred to as the Kuznets inverted-U curve, which we discussed earlier in this chapter and in the previous one.

In a pathbreaking study of global inequality between 1820 and 1992, François Bourguignon and Christian Morrisson found confirmation of these trends. Their study was novel in that they rejected the then customary hypothesis that all citizens within a country would receive the same average income. Their work was all the more challenging because they did not have household survey data for the 1820–1960 period and so had to work with quantile shares of per capita GDP data. Whereas empirical studies of international growth ignored income disparities within countries and limited themselves to measuring only between-country inequality, Bourguignon and Morrisson were able to count both dimensions, thus offering a less biased analysis of global inequality. By counting both dimensions, moreover, they showed that global inequality is higher than implied by measures based only on between-country inequality.[48] The Gini coefficient of population-weighted international inequality (that is, based on average per capita GDPs) for 1820, for example, was 16.

Bourguignon and Morrisson underscore that by simply introducing within-country income disparities into the calculation, the Gini coefficient increases to 50.

The Gini coefficient, when calculated this way, shows that global inequality was already high when the Industrial Revolution was under way in England and beginning to spread to other European countries and their offshoots. Milanovic likened the Industrial Revolution to "a big bang that launched a part of mankind onto a path of higher incomes and sustained growth, while the majority stayed where they were, and some even went down."[49] In the century between 1820 and the eve of the First World War, according to Bourguignon and Morrisson, the global Gini index rose from 50 to 61, and it rose again, although less quickly, to 64 in 1950.[50] For the period after 1950, opinions differ. According to Bourguignon and Morrisson, the Gini coefficient continued to grow, although at a lesser pace. Milanovic, on the contrary, recorded a lower level for 1988, but at the same time noticed a slightly higher value for the early 1990s. In a 2016 study, Christoph Lakner and Branko Milanovic offered Gini coefficients for the most recent period, 1988–2008. Table 4.2 summarizes the evolution of the global Gini coefficient according to these three studies. Of note, Lakner and Milanovic's values are higher than previously published values. This is because their data set includes many more countries and many more income groups for each country, and also because of differences in the purchasing power parity (PPP) surveys used in earlier studies and more recent ones (1990 and 2005 PPP surveys, respectively).[51]

Although the time period he covered was much more limited, from a methodological point of view Milanovic's 2002 article was also groundbreaking, as it was entirely based on household surveys; that is, for the first time, world income distribution was calculated the same way as we would calculate a national income

Table 4.2. Global income inequality, 1820–2008 (Gini index)

	1820	1850	1870	1890	1910	1929	1950	1960	1970	1980	1988	1992	1993	1998	2003	2008
Bourguignon-Morrisson	50.0	53.2	56.0	58.8	61.0	61.6	64.0	63.5	65.0	65.7		65.7				
Milanovic											62.6		66.0			
Lakner-Milanovic											72.2		71.9	71.5	71.9	70.5

Sources: François Bourguignon and Christian Morrisson, "Inequality among World Citizens: 1820–1992," *American Economic Review* 92, no. 4 (2002), pp. 727–44; Branko Milanovic, "True World Income Distribution, 1988 and 1993: First Calculation Based on Household Surveys Alone," *Economic Journal* 112, no. 476 (2002), pp. 51–92; and Christoph Lakner and Branko Milanovic, "Global Income Distribution: From the Fall of the Berlin Wall to the Great Recession," *World Bank Economic Review* 30, no. 2 (2016), pp. 203–32.

distribution from regional, subnational surveys.[52] As noted in the appendix, household surveys are increasingly commonly used as a fundamental source of data, though they present some problems in terms of consistency and comparability.

We can conclude that by the late 1960s and the early 1970s, the growth of European countries and their former temperate colonies had slowed, while other countries, especially in Asia, were catching up. Starting in the 1980s, in particular, China's economic performance began to hugely affect global inequality trends because of China's very large demographic weight (India followed approximately twenty years later).

In a nutshell, then, for almost two centuries the world witnessed the increasing spread of globalization, which was characterized by many elements and, from the perspective of inequality trends, by two major facts: first, increasing between-country inequality (or among groups of countries, such as the European industrializing countries versus the nonindustrializing countries), and second, decreasing inequality within countries, either because the countries were poor and thus the "inequality possibility frontier" remained relatively low or because countries were industrializing and, after an initial phase of increasing domestic inequality, found themselves on the downward portion of the Kuznets curve.

These are therefore the centuries when the so-called citizenship premium blossomed in full. In 1820, within-country inequality accounted for the lion's share of global inequality, 70 per cent, against a mere 30 per cent that was due to between-country inequality. By the mid-twentieth century, however, the proportion had more than reversed: 80 per cent of total global inequality reflected between-country inequality, whereas only 20 per cent was attributable to within-county disparities.[53] In other words, from a global perspective, whereas in 1820 it was crucial to be born into the right family (that is, a rich family) and one's country of birth was only of secondary importance, since the mid-twentieth century the opposite has been true, and country of birth has become the major determinant of where individuals stay in the global distribution of income. This is why the phenomenon of huge international migrations with which we opened this chapter is a structural phenomenon of our era, and this is why opposing it with barbed-wire walls and fences (such as those on the US–Mexican border and the border between Hungary and Serbia and Croatia) is short-sighted and ultimately ineffectual. The only foreseeable effect of these demagogic solutions is a rise in the number of individuals who will lose their lives attempting to migrate.[54]

Compared to the previous trends, the third globalizing wave is completely different. Older processes seem to have reversed: since the 1980s, between-country inequality, although still very high, has begun to subside, while within-country inequality seems to be on the rise. Caution is necessary here, though. First, because the inversion in the trends is very recent, it may well be that a new inversion will follow, taking us back to the well-known trends of increasing between-country divergence and decreasing within-country inequality. In that case, the "new trend" of the third globalizing wave would best be viewed as a temporary, exceptional event. Second, the delineation of trends may be incorrect because of the usual problems arising from measurements and comparison issues by different investigators (grounded in the use of different data sets, parameters, and samples).

With these caveats in mind, however, it is worth analyzing in more detail what appears at the moment to be a major U-turn in global inequality dynamics. The U-turn refers to the shape of the Kuznets curve. Apparently, the theory according to which inequality would be low at low levels of income, would then grow during industrialization, would reach a plateau, and would then decrease at higher levels of income and mass consumption proved more or less correct for the first and second globalizing waves but needs an important update for the present day. If we complement table 4.1 with more recent data on within-country inequality we obtain table 4.3, which shows that the Kuznets curve does not stop at the (final) trough but is starting to move upward again. For this reason, Milanovic has spoken of a reclined S, like this: ∿, and has more recently proposed renaming the Kuznets curve as Kuznets "waves" (we already observed an undulating trajectory in the case of Chile in table 4.1).[55] The data are less than conclusive. For example, Brazil has shown a constant decrease at least until 2012; the Netherlands have shown only a modest increase of two Gini points since 1982; and Japan has basically remained at its 1962 level. These trends, however, do not necessarily undermine the hypothesis of Kuznets waves, as they may simply relate to a lack of synchronicity between countries. What we know for certain is that in many countries, inequality has started to rise again.

James K. Galbraith notes that the recent upward movement in inequality in the United States and a few other rich countries does not contradict the basic Kuznets hypothesis. The fundamental point in Kuznets's analysis was that change in pay inequality largely depended on major sectoral changes in the economy. The transition from a predominantly agrarian to an industrial economy caused industrial incomes to rise, and inequality first increased (in the middle of the transition) and later decreased (when the transition had been completed). The technological revolution that has been unfolding since the 1980s in information technology and the service and financial sectors is a crucial new structural change, and accordingly it has widened income disparities again. The Kuznets mechanism, in other words, has started

Table 4.3. Kuznets waves, as proposed by Milanovic (years and Gini coefficients)[a]

COUNTRY	INITIAL POINT		PEAK		TROUGH		NEWLY UPWARD TREND	
	YEAR	GINI	YEAR	GINI	YEAR	GINI	YEAR	GINI
United States	1774	45	1933	50	1979	35	2013	42
United Kingdom	1688	45	1867	58	1962	28	2010	36
Spain	1850	38	1953	54	1985	31	2010	35
Italy[b]	n.a.	n.a.	1860	51	1983	30	2010	36
Netherlands	1561	55	1732	62	1982	28	2010	30

Source: Milanovic, *Global Inequality*, pp. 70–91, reporting data from the same sources listed in table 4.1.

a. For the more recent upward movement in the Kuznets waves, we have refrained from defining the year and the Gini coefficient as the "peak" year as we still don't know whether and for how long this upward trend will last.

b. Data availability for Italy starts at the time of political unification, in 1861, and follows a continuous downward trend; therefore, no initial trough data are available.

over, no longer as a consequence of the first industrial revolution but of the technological revolution of the late twentieth century.[56]

Interestingly, Galbraith has reached these results through a very different approach to data collection and calculation, originating in his dissatisfaction with the limitations of household surveys in terms of costs, complexity, and the availability of reliable and comparable data (more on this in the appendix).

If the hypothesis of a new rise in the Kuznets curve in connection to a new technological revolution is correct, the United States appears to be a particularly relevant case to study, both because of the significant size of its population, and thus of its influence on global inequality trends, and because of its leading role among industrial economies. It has been argued that a "perfect storm" of inequality may be approaching what has long been considered the land of opportunity. A combination of capital and income concentration is making the US income distribution increasingly skewed. The top-incomes have constantly grown, while the incomes of the middle class have lagged behind for decades, and this trend seems to be increasingly strong.

What is new, at least at the global level, is that inequality in another large country, China, seems to have stopped growing, with the Chinese Gini index around 47–48 since the turn of the twenty-first century or slightly thereafter. This major change in the most populated country of the world, together with the high economic growth experienced by a number of other populous Asian countries since the 1980s, has driven global income inequality down. From the late 1980s to the turn of the twenty-first century, global inequality remained relatively stable at slightly above a Gini index of 65 or 70 (depending on whether we use Bourguignon-Morrisson data or Lakner-Milanovic data; however, these differences in the absolute value of the Gini index do not affect the general trend). After 2000, global inequality began to decrease, mainly due to the momentous growth of China and India. Because of its internal dynamics, up to 2000 China was "the great income equalizer." After 2000, India joined China in this role, and global inequality began its downward trend.[57]

The role of populous Asian countries should make us reflect on the geographic spread of this apparent global income convergence. Concepts of inequality unweighted for population are of some use here, as they deflate the preponderance of China's and India's influence on global inequality dynamics by not taking their huge populations into consideration. International inequality trends unweighted for population have actually shown growing inequality until 2000, when inequality stabilized, beginning to diminish only in the mid-2000s.[58] This means that at the global level, whereas highly populated countries have driven inequality down, entire regions have not participated in this trend. Latin America, Eastern Europe, and Africa have increasingly diverged from the rich world, and Africa has experienced an especially bad performance.

The combination of diminishing within-country inequality in large Asian countries and increasing within-country inequality in a number of rich countries, especially the United States, has important global consequences. The richest 1 per cent of any country's population has obviously benefited everywhere, taking an increasingly larger slice of the pie. Among the beneficiaries of this phenomenon, however, is also the emerging middle class in China, India, Thailand, Vietnam, and Indonesia, where, of course, the middle class would be considered poor if compared in absolute terms with the middle class of Western economies. The great losers, in this global reshuffle, are those belonging to the lower middle class of rich countries, whose real incomes, in the last twenty-five years, have grown slowly or remained stagnant.[59] Figure 4.2, which some scholars call the "elephant curve" for its resemblance to an elephant with an upward trunk, shows this process vividly.

Figure 4.2 shows how different ventiles fared in per cent income gains in the two decades between the twentieth and the twenty-first century. Point *A* corresponds to the global "1 per cent," or the global rich (there are at least a few plutocrats everywhere). Point *B* corresponds to people who belong approximately to the 80th percentile of global income distribution. The vast majority of them are the old middle class of the historically rich countries of Western Europe, North America, and Oceania, with the addition of Japan. They fared rather well during the

Figure 4.2. Relative gain in real per capita income by global income level, 1988–2008

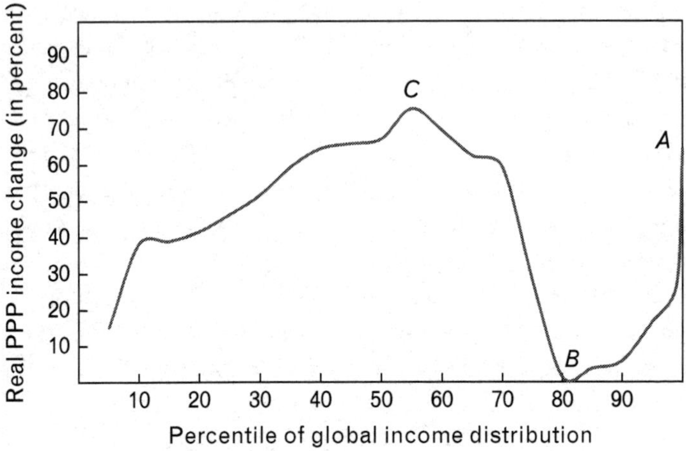

Source: Branko Milanovic, *Global Inequality: A New Approach for the Age of Globalization* (Belknap Press of Harvard University Press, 2016), p. 11.

twentieth century, but the dramatic news is that their real income has grown basically not at all for two decades. Point *C*, finally, corresponds to those who have gained the most from the recent globalizing wave, and nine-tenths of them live in China and other East Asian countries. They belong to the middle of the income distribution of their own countries, and they have witnessed their real income grow fastest at the global level.

This still relatively poor emerging "global middle class" is the actual winner of the current globalizing wave. This goes a long way toward explaining what is happening politically in economically advanced countries, where economic mobility has stopped. The increasingly skewed distribution within the rich countries of Western Europe, North America, Australia, New Zealand, and

Japan, combined with many other aspects of the current globalizing wave, plays an important role in the mounting discontent expressed toward globalization, international cooperation, trade openness, and even humanitarian openness that is erupting in liberal democracies. The inability of the state to govern the transnational forces of globalization, coupled with the stagnation of some sectors of rich countries' populations, is fueling social discontent, reactionary political movements, and demagogic ideas. Increasing inequality, in other words, is directly affecting and changing for the worse the social cohesion of liberal democracies and the way these democracies function. Chapter 5 takes up this question.

FIVE

Inequality and Democracy: An Open Issue

Does democracy have a genetic basis?
"When not sure about a direction of travel, wild olive baboons vote democratically."

Ariana Strandburg-Peshkin and others, *Science*[1]

As discussed in chapters 2 and 3, economic inequality per se has never been central to the concerns of economics as a discipline. Among the reasons for the limited scholarly attention to inequality is surely the pervasive academic belief that an egalitarian distribution might prove detrimental to production through its effects on saving. Since the rich save more, and since, according to conventional wisdom, savings go toward financing real capital accumulation, lesser amounts of resources owned by the rich would turn into less investment, less production, and less subsequent income: a shrinking of the pie. Thus most economists in the past preferred to focus on growth rather than on personal distribution, and when the plight of the poor could no longer be ignored, concern shifted to how to improve their material condition. How to enlarge employment opportunities and how to promote growth thus became the target of theorizing since the aim was to enlarge the pie rather than to make its slices more equal, in the expectation that a larger pie would mean larger slices for everybody. This reasoning hinged on the notion that it is the absolute rather than the relative dimension of the slice that matters. This view is definitely challenged today.

Economic research has only recently become interested in the *personal* distribution of incomes, and one of the reasons – if not the main one – is that economically developed countries are now experiencing an alarming degree of inequality. Prolonged unemployment, wage dispersion, an increasing accumulation of wealth by the few coincident with stagnant incomes for the rest, a steeper social ladder, and a tightening access to education because of more difficult financial conditions are the main factors that have brought the personal distribution of income to center stage in the twenty-first century. Moreover, globalization has not yielded what it promised to in terms of growth and equality among countries, and it affects in important ways economic and distributional processes within countries.

Thus economic inequality is at the forefront of political debate today, arguably because social movements have emerged that forced economists to turn their attention to this issue. To explain this shift in focus, we must first undertake a brief exploration of the complex links between inequality and democracy, focusing on the effects of the former on the latter.[2]

IS THERE A CONNECTION BETWEEN INEQUALITY AND DEMOCRACY?

Democracy, like inequality, is a difficult concept to define. Inequality requires attributes and value judgments before it can have any real meaning, and there can be no complete agreement on the concept of democracy, which may be shaped by different social and political agendas.

A starting point for assessing any linkage between equality and democracy may be to question whether political equality – which has a central place in any theory of democracy – entails economic equality. The answer seems to be no.

There is no necessary causal connection between the two concepts except that the absence of political equality makes the issue of economic equality irrelevant. How could honest concerns about differences in the economic condition of people be possible in a world where people do not even have equality in their *political* condition? Concurrently, scholars of democracy firmly state that democracy, in both its ancient and modern version, never promised economic equality.[3] Democracy promises *political* equality, and economic and social inequality are not expected to convert necessarily into political inequality.[4]

Though not necessarily, they can convert, however. In fact, a substantial degree of economic inequality may corrupt political equality or slow the realization of its potential, even in a democratic regime. As a result, political processes may in turn reinforce inequality. An alarming feedback loop might therefore get established, and some form of oligarchy might be the outcome of this deterioration of democracy.

Exactly this is at the forefront of the current political and economic debate: the role that inequality plays in rich and well-established democracies, where the increasing concentration of wealth in a few hands prompts serious fears for the health of democratic institutions. That is the topic of this chapter.

UNDERSTANDING DEMOCRACY

Demos-kratos – government by the people – is a broad conceptual area where different institutional arrangements and sets of values can coexist. Although an in-depth discussion of what democracy exceeds the scope of the present chapter, if we want to understand the complex relationship between inequality and democracy, a few words on how democracies are supposed to work are in order.[5]

In particular, to make progress in suggesting how economic inequality can degrade democracy, we must first investigate what the modern concept of democracy is, since it is certainly something different and broader than universal suffrage only. Regular elections and majority rule no longer suffice to define democracy. Likewise, egalitarianism, expressed by equality with respect to voting, laws, and rights, is no longer considered a sufficient basis for the proper functioning of a democracy. Advanced capitalist societies are complex entities in which many diverse institutions interact and in which citizens have many channels beyond elections (associational, partisan, functional, territorial, collective, individual, and so on) to make their voices heard, and to participate in democratic processes.[6]

Robert Dahl, one of the most influential scholars of democracy, is a fundamental reference for our analysis. Specifically, Dahl introduces the concept of "polyarchy," or "polyarchic democracy," as the modern type of democratic government. In *On Democracy* he lists six major institutions of polyarchy (some having subcategories) and explains their foundational role with respect to democracy. Dahl conceives of polyarchy as a "political order" characterized by (we reword slightly) (1) the election of officials, (2) free, fair, and frequent elections, (3) freedom of expression, (4) viable alternative sources of information, (5) associational autonomy, and (6) inclusive citizenship. All the institutions are necessary – though not sufficient – for having a democratic process in the governance of a country. These institutions represent the raw material for the five criteria that have to be met for political equality to obtain, namely, (1) effective participation, (2) voting equality, (3) enlightened understanding, (4) control of the agenda, and (5) the inclusion of adults. Dahl writes, "To the extent that any of the requirements is violated, the members will not be politically equal."[7] As Dahl suggests, these are standard criteria for evaluating the democratic performance of political institutions and serve as guides for shaping and reshaping them.[8] Many variations of Dahl's scheme exist, with additional institutions, enlargements, and refinements, which have led to a "thick" conception of democracy.[9]

Once democracy has been established with its basic formal requisites, the quality of that democracy can be examined. Larry Diamond and Leonardo Morlino propose eight dimensions, so intertwined as to be difficult to distinguish one from another, on which the quality of democracy can vary. Five of them are considered mainly procedural: the rule of law, participation, competition, vertical accountability, and horizontal accountability. Two are substantive: respect for civil and political freedoms, and the progressive implementation of greater political equality. The last one, responsiveness, bridges procedure and substance.[10]

DOES INEQUALITY UNDERMINE DEMOCRACY?

Whenever any of these eight qualitative dimensions is not fully realized, inequality can arise even in an already well-settled democracy. When they are scant or nonexistent, some basic requirements for active citizenship, such as access to information and knowledge, are seriously weakened. Uninformed people cannot fully exercise their political rights; the increasing technocratic bent of society, which more and more favors *the experts*, tends to mute the voices of whole segments of the population, marginalizing them; the progressive concentration of the media in the hands of a few reduces the pluralism of information, while the emergence of a uniform voice lowers the quality of that information. Even democratic societies tend to be monopolized by rich and powerful segments of the population in pursuit of their own interests. This kind of evolution toward a weakening of active citizenship is more likely to occur when, for instance, the rule of law is weak, effective participation beyond voting is not favored (and sometimes obstacles are erected against voting participation), access to the political arena is limited, and behavioral opacity exists both within the government and national and local bureaucracies and between elected representatives and electors.

Similarly, the same disadvantaged segments of population can be particularly hit in their freedom by the incomplete implementation of essential social rights, such as the rights associated with employment. The same segments of the population may have a deficit in political equality because of fewer opportunities to participate in political life, no chance whatsoever to influence either public debate or collective preferences, and no chance to control the government's agenda. A deficit of effective participation arises if a part of the population is cut off from the modalities through which collective decisions are made, and this in turn determines what policies are actually adopted.

Those same mechanisms do not affect the rich, who have many ways of protecting their status and interests. As Edward Glaeser writes, "The rich can influence political outcomes through lobbying activities or membership in interest groups ... or bribing judges ... or making a mockery of popular democracy."[11] This is what Daron Acemoglu, Simon Johnson, and James A. Robinson distinguish as de jure versus de facto political power, with the former formally defined by the political institutions of a society and the latter arising from an informal but nonetheless essential negotiation between political actors.[12] Even in societies characterized by formally democratic institutions (granting de jure political power to all), only affluent people and the elites have de facto power, being able to shape political institutions through their current influence. The political equality required by democracy is thus seriously damaged, and we can answer the question with which this section opened in the positive: Yes, inequality potentially undermines democracy.

If so, two interesting questions arise: What are the consequences? And do they matter?

What the consequences are depends on a crucial dimension of the quality of democracy mentioned above: responsiveness. If governments respond to people and make and implement policies that the citizens want, the degree of legitimacy will be high and the socio-political identity of the polity strong.[13] If they do not, many scenarios are possible: an estrangement of individuals from societal life, open opposition to rulers, social unrest, even riots. So, once again, the consequences of inequality do matter.

The lack of responsiveness is destined to leave a political mark, since it leads to a deterioration of citizens' trust in institutions and to a progressive estrangement from political life and participation in it. The loss of legitimacy in the eyes of citizens caused by the failure of democratic institutions to work properly weakens the state itself and opens the door to antidemocratic impulses. As Aristotle and Machiavelli remind us, a state is infinitely stronger if rulers are trusted by the people, since disillusionment and decreasing participation leave empty spaces in which oligarchy can flourish. Or, as Jeffrey A. Winters puts it, a "civil oligarchy" can arise: a situation in which oligarchs become increasingly powerful, and yet "strong and impersonal systems of law dominate oligarchs rather than oligarchs dominating (or being) the law."[14] In other words, an intermediate situation can develop in which power is centered more and more on the interests of the few while still being ostensibly exercised within a democratic framework.

This transitional situation, however, is intrinsically unstable, as "the gradual erosion of freedoms, guarantees, and processes that are vital to democracy" causes what Guillermo O'Donnell has described as the "slow strangulation of democracy by insidious oligarchy."[15] The renowned political theorist Adam Przeworski underscores this point when he asserts, "Democracy endures only if it is self-enforcing."[16]

SOME EMPIRICS

Political theory has been suggesting at length that inequality should level automatically in a democratic setting – or slow down sensibly rather than surge – through the working of what is called the median voter mechanism. The most straightforward prediction of this famous suggestion, one of the outcomes of "public choice" theory, is that income redistribution becomes popular when the mean income is higher than the income of the median voter.[17] According to this theory, in a democratic system the combination of taxes and transfers will be the one preferred by the voter who stays exactly in the middle of the distribution: the voter who has the median income. Since the empirical distributions in all advanced economies exhibit a median income lower than the mean, the higher the economic inequality is, the higher the combination of taxes and transfers in the preferences of the median voter should be. Thus, in a majoritarian democracy, it has to be expected that high inequality will gradually smooth out.

Besides some theoretical objections,[18] this prediction has not been validated by facts: either redistribution did not take place or it was insufficient to prevent inequality from surging.[19] Failure of the theory to play out as predicted could result from two different causes. First, in the real world, democracy used to coexist with a non-negligible degree of inequality, and this occurrence has never been depicted as evil: the dominance of trickle-down economic arguments – what happens at the top helps growth, and growth helps everybody – made inequality a much less important issue than growth. A second possible explanation lies in political accountability. When inequality persists (or increases), "the electors" are not the poor or low- and middle-income citizens since, if they were, politicians would actively behave in ways intended to mitigate their unfavorable conditions. If this does not happen, it means that redistribution is avoided on purpose since wealth concentration has reverberated into politics. However, empirical validation of the transmutation of socioeconomic inequality into political inequality is lacking: though everybody is convinced that money affects politics, political theorists argue that the role of nonpolitical resources in shaping political outcomes is not proved.[20] In fact – and unfortunately – political scientists are ill-equipped to take up this task because of the near impossibility of measuring democracy and its quality, and consequently the relationship between economic inequality and the quality of democracy remains more a matter of speculation than of empirical observation. Nonetheless, some results, particularly by Larry Bartels, are noteworthy. For instance, there is evidence that the rich have great influence on the behavior of elected officials while people in the bottom third of the income distribution seem to have no impact, and, in general, political leaders appear to react to what middle- and upper-income citizens prefer.[21]

Later research confirmed Bartels's findings: responsiveness exists, but it is tilted toward the most affluent citizens, which overlaps with the narrative by Paul Krugman and Jacob Hacker and Paul Pierson.[22] They all tell a (particularly American) story of the progressive strengthening of the rich elites and a consequent bending of public interest to the private interests of the wealthy, a finding that stresses, ironically, how the winner-take-all aspects of the economy are clearly not determined by the so quintessentially American "free-market" mechanism. Politics plays a fundamental role in the winner-take-all logic.

Thus, responsiveness as a quality of democracy – which is what the above-mentioned studies more or less explicitly point to – appears weak, and when responsiveness is weak, citizens' reaction is difficult to anticipate, as is the evolution of the democratic political system that might turn into less democratic scenarios.

THE SOCIAL COST OF INEQUALITY AND ITS REVERBERATION ON DEMOCRACY

The supposed inverse relationship between inequality and (the quality of) democracy appears even more nefarious when one considers the self-sustaining mechanism acting through the purely social consequences of economic disparities.

A 2009 study by Richard G. Wilkinson and Kate Pickett provides evidence of the impressive correlation between inequality and social disadvantage in a wide sample of rich and industrialized countries.[23] More unequal countries do worse on almost every quality-of-life indicator, such as level of trust, mental health, life expectancy, infant mortality, obesity, children's educational performance, teenage birth rate, homicide rate, imprisonment rate, and social mobility. Wilkinson and Pickett's message is clear: if social problems were caused by material life conditions, the more affluent countries should perform better than the less affluent ones (still in the same group of rich countries). Instead the evidence suggests that it is the relative position of individuals and groups within a society that matters the most: where income differences are bigger, social distances are bigger too, and social stratification is stronger. When inequality grows, the differences between population groups strengthen. Eventually, what distinguishes these groups is their social distance. This distance can reach enormous proportions and can lead to social exclusion through disparities in the consumption sphere, in health and housing conditions, in access to education and to the labour market, in the social relations network (so-called social capital), and in social mobility. Though it is not the only cause of social stratification, income inequality has a crucial impact on it.

These aspects have recently drawn investigators' attention because of the greater collective awareness of the risks of growing inequality.[24] The ills of society are perceived more and more as threats to social cohesion and political structures. Among the potential drivers of inequality, three seem particularly relevant: health care, education provision, and social mobility. Whereas income inequality undoubtedly affects health inequality, the inverse correlation is less strong. Of course, health inequality is a fundamental issue, representing perhaps the greatest social injustice.[25] And yet it does not seem to directly affect disparities in income except in less developed countries, where chronic malnutrition and illnesses prevent people from earning a living. In the case of education provision and social mobility the correlation with inequality works both ways: when they are missing, income inequality increases, and when income inequality is high, education provision and social mobility decrease.

When inequality is high, education cannot play its role of social equalizer. Access to high-level schooling for low-income (and low-education) families is narrowed, if not virtually suppressed, because they are excluded from the credit market. Moreover, the rich often resist funding public schooling through taxes, leading to a generalized underfunding of public educational institutions. For instance, public spending on education is on average lower in countries such as Britain and the United States, where the rich participate more in the political process than the poor, and higher in countries such as Sweden and Denmark, where levels of political participation are approximately similar across the income scale. Simple speculation – or, if you prefer, Aristotle's 2,000-year-old argument that the poor are in the grip of demagogues – suggests that low-educated people may more easily become victims of political manipulation and less interested in the functioning of the institutions of democracy: a process that contributes to lowering the quality of democracy.

Just as happens for education, lower social mobility often turns into a trap, with shrinking of opportunities unambiguously demonstrated empirically. In the case of the United States, for example, Alan Krueger, economist and former chairman of the Council of Economic Advisers, has recently proposed what he imaginatively labeled the "Great Gatsby curve," recalling Gatsby's difficulties in climbing the social ladder despite his wealth.[26] Krueger was referring to the relationship between inequality and generational earning mobility, technically known as intergenerational elasticity in earnings (IGE), which is the percentage difference in earnings in the child's generation associated with the percentage difference in the parental generation. This relationship is positive: increasing IGE and increasing inequality go together. But an increasing IGE represents a society with decreasing mobility since a value of 0.6, for instance, "tells us that if one father makes 100% more than another then the son of the high income father will, as an adult, earn 60% more than the son of the relatively lower income father. An elasticity of 0.2 says this 100% difference between the fathers would only lead to a 20% difference between the sons. A lower elasticity means a society with more mobility."[27] Recent studies put the IGE for the United States at around 0.4 in 2012.

The intergenerational persistence of disadvantages impedes any positive evolution for the lowest strata of society and locks them into immobile stratification. At the same time, it contributes to reinforcing the negative influences of social disadvantage on the democratic political environment. The power of the uppermost tier of society, the elites, expands, and the vicious circle continues onward through a self-reinforcing mechanism. It is true that democracy per se never promised social mobility or equality in education, but it is also true that both social mobility and equality have historically been achieved within a democratic framework, through state actions aimed at removing social barriers. Today, egalitarian government policies are less and less effective. Thus, the question becomes: Can people be politically equal if they are socially unequal?

Inevitably, socioeconomic inequality percolates through the political realm as, in the words of Bartels, "wealthier and better-educated citizens are more likely than the poor and less-educated to have clearly formulated and well-informed preferences, and significantly more likely to turn out to vote, to have direct contact with public officials, and to contribute money and energy to political campaigns."[28]

Economic and social power easily convert into political power, in the specific form of a wealth-driven power, or plutocracy. Whenever individuals have a different capacity for exercising equal political rights, as seems often to be the case, the condition of political equality is violated.[29] In this regard, it is easy to imagine that the advantage provided by census can become so relevant as to crowd out the middle- and low-income citizens from active participation. Here again a self-reinforcing mechanism is evident as middle- and low-income citizens feel impotent, frustrated, and excluded from any decisionmaking process. As a result, the spirit of citizenship is deeply undermined. The evidence that nearly all the forms of public participation in political processes – for example, voting turnouts – are now in decline in most Western countries points in the direction of deteriorating institutions.[30] Moreover, the underlying degree of morality of politicians and rulers is increasingly questioned, and a sharp reduction in trust in turn causes lack of political and electoral participation. The more that ordinary people keep far from centers of power, political agendas, and governmental actions, the less their interests are represented and supported and the more others' interests are. Again, the political institutional framework tends to bend more and more toward oligarchy.

THE ECONOMIC EFFECTS OF ECONOMIC INEQUALITY

Since it is undeniable that growth is a sort of prerequisite to an overall improvement in living conditions, we must ascertain whether inequality is harmful or beneficial to growth. As it happens, the effects of inequality on growth are still heatedly debated, and the "old wave" of arguments holding that inequality (or at least a certain degree of it) is not harmful, even if not beneficial to growth, has not completely disappeared.

The earlier argument that the pursuit of equality harms economic growth through various disincentive mechanisms can be read as the flip side of saying that poverty rather than unbalanced distribution is the problem: "Poverty bothers me. Inequality does not. I just don't care," Willem H. Buiter said.[31] Though worrying about poverty is absolutely just and important, caring only about the extreme bottom can result in locking in the current personal distribution of income and wealth. The underlying philosophy of being supportive of an unbalanced income and wealth distribution was (and partially still is) the usual trickle-down argument, and the main concern is still, as ever, the size of the pie. The traditional view maintained that inequality increased aggregate savings, which in turn increased investment and GDP growth. This theoretical causal chain, however, is not as robust as it might seem. The direct linkage between saving and capital accumulation has been questioned since the 1930s, in particular by John Maynard Keynes, who stressed the crucial role of expectations in determining the demand for real capital. Moreover, even within a framework of optimistic expectations, the inertial behavior of the banking and financial sectors – often more inclined to financial speculation than to supporting the activity of firms (at least those without sizable collateral) – can become a formidable obstacle to the process of capital accumulation. Savings, in other words, are not per se a sufficient condition for investment.

The economic mainstream, however, also holds that in a highly egalitarian framework, incentives thin out, and the total amount of productive effort in the economy decreases, making all, including the poor, worse off than in a less egalitarian context.

Insofar as it is "just" to discern each person's contribution to society, inequality is judged to be not unjust. According to this view, in a market economy inequality reflects the true abilities or inabilities of people and the "natural" differences among them, provided (at least in the democratic version of this line of thought) that they are given equality of opportunity by the state. As noted in chapter 2, this position found its manifesto in Milton Friedman's 1953 article, with his assessment that "individual choice through the market can greatly modify the effect on the personal distribution of income both of circumstances outside the control of individuals concerned and of collective actions designed to affect the distribution of income," such as taxation and subsidies.[32]

Finally, the mainstream perspective holds that taxes and transfers implemented according to any kind of median voter theory have a distortionary effect and slow down the pace of growth.

But is this perspective still unquestioned in economics? Clearly, the undeniable social cost of inequality is currently affecting how economists conceive of the relationship between inequality and economic growth. Economics now seems to be turning away from the earlier argument that the pursuit of equality harms economic growth through various disincentive mechanisms. Inequality is becoming increasingly relevant for the economics discipline since it appears potentially dangerous for *technical* reasons.

When inequality becomes extreme, it ceases to be "useful" in any possible way for growth, insofar as it almost paralyzes the functioning of the economy. Simply put, whereas low profits reduce the level of investment and lead to stagnation, high profits, combined with falling wages, lead to weak demand for consumer goods (unless consumer credit sustains demand). This latter circumstance leads to depressed expectations on the firms' side, discouraging their interest in real investment and increasing their drive toward financial speculation. This situation is much more likely to occur when the high incomes at the top of the distribution go to the working rich, that is, top managers who are not themselves owners of the capital but work for a capitalist, who is usually hidden from the public eye. The squeeze on wages combined with the surge in high incomes at the top is an unequivocal sign of where financial surpluses are channeled, as well as of the increased role of the banking system and the financial sector in general. Their increasingly strong influence on the policymaking process conduces inevitably to deregulation and less progressive fiscal policies. This split between the enrichment of the few and the interest of the great many eventually sabotages growth itself. Since the 1980s, the slowdown in economic growth and productivity in the world's leading economies has become almost a constant, contributing to the onset of instability: the pie has grown less than expected, or it has outright shrunk.

The endogenous growth theory of the 1990s – from Lucas to Romer through the anticipatory insight of Becker – contributed theoretically to alter the traditional old line of thought. Hinging on the consideration that human capital is as important as (if not more important than) real capital, it brought education to the forefront. If education becomes pivotal for growth, and if surging inequality means shrinking opportunities for people, schooling undergoes a huge transformation, and not for the better: it becomes too expensive for low-income families and less relevant for the low-educated ones, who often are the same families. When credit constraint binds people without tangible assets in their borrowing capacity so that they cannot invest in human capital, inequality seriously hampers growth, and the mechanism easily becomes self-reinforcing through the lock-in effect: the more a society is divided in terms of income and wealth, the more reluctant the rich are to spend money on society. Thus, studies in the 1990s repeatedly showed that the answer to the question, "Does inequality within a country slow its growth?," is likely to be positive, though the direction of causality appears not so easy to ascertain.[33] Besides the findings that greater inequality lowers economic growth and that countries with less inequality tend to experience higher and less volatile growth, these pieces of literature eventuate that not only is the trickle-down argument contradicted (since the rich lobby for policies that are beneficial to them but that may harm the rest of the economy), there is also some evidence that equality "protects" democracy.[34] Less unequal societies actually look more stable politically – in part because a still strong middle class is actively engaged in political life – and better able to smooth out the negative effects of external shocks on growth.[35] Thus, in addition to not directly enhancing growth, inequality seems to have an indirect negative effect as well, for whenever it hits democracy, it also diminishes the potentially tutorial role that democracy has on growth. This role becomes evident in all those aspects that are reputed to be important for growth, such as the rule of law, widespread education, and a high level of publicly supplied services.[36] Therefore, the linkage between inequality and democracy is also strengthened through growth: if inequality obstructs or slows down growth, some of the constituencies of a democracy weaken. "We do not measure trust in our national income accounts, but investments in trust are no less important than those in human capital or machines," writes Joseph Stiglitz.[37]

As is obvious, the fight on whether empirical findings corroborate this analytical reorientation is in full swing. A number of scholars, even on the center left of the political spectrum, have suggested caution in claiming that inequality is necessarily detrimental to growth, opting for a more nuanced position;

the relationship is nonlinear and as such it can go either way.[38] Salvatore Morelli, for example, has recently argued that inequality in principle can contribute to create macroeconomic instability, though "no relationships have been robustly demonstrated without qualification."[39] In a similar vein, Dani Rodrik has commented that "the relationship between equality and economic performance is likely to be contingent rather than fixed, depending on the deeper causes of inequality and many mediating factors;" hence, "we should not invert the error and conclude that greater equality and better economic performance always go together. After all, there really is only one universal truth in economics: It depends."[40] And yet, if this truth may apply to economics, and if sound and sophisticated economic analysis is essential for informed policymaking, one must remain aware that we are not dealing here with mere technicalities: as we discuss in the next section, politics (and most notably equality-related politics) will always remain a contentious field.

IS INEQUALITY UNAVOIDABLE TODAY?

If economic inequality is socially undesirable and politically dangerous since it threatens democracy by insinuating itself into the realm of political equality, the interesting question becomes: Is economic inequality compatible with democracy, and if not, can we privilege democracy? And furthermore, is inequality inevitable?

Unfortunately, it appears to be inevitable. The unavoidability of inequality rests on the nature of the market economy and the "there-is-no-alternative" attitude toward it. However, the outcomes of market capitalism often differ from its textbook descriptions as an efficient system for allocating resources. Some people become "naturally" disadvantaged because, for instance, their employment condition is inferior to their skills, owing to some managerial decision, or coordination failure, or institutional weakness. Moreover, their unemployment or depletion or illness is beyond their control, and nobody protects them. The market economy generates naturally unbalanced monetary resources, and generates at the same time a disparity in the access to information and to political elites through a wide spectrum of differences in social status and education. To the degree that democracy needs the market, and politics fails to control the free-market operating rules, democracy ends up cohabitating with economic inequality: they can be compatible.

Redistribution is certainly possible, though not redistribution of everything. For instance, the structural dependence on capital makes even politicians on the left cautious about imposing a heavy burden on powerful industrial economic interests.[41] Again, the equalization of human capital through investment in education does not automatically equalize subsequent earnings, which also depend on other features, such as social background. As Adam Przeworski has written, "Some degree of economic inequality is just inevitable. Democracy is impotent against it, but so is every other conceivable political arrangement."[42]

If market capitalism is unavoidable, if it inevitably generates some degree of economic inequality (or, worse, if inequality is innate to capitalism, as Thomas Piketty's *Capital in the Twenty-First Century* ultimately argues), and if economic inequality can allow democracy to deteriorate, what can we do?

At least, we can understand the present in the awareness of all the dangerous connections we have been overlooking: inequality can be tolerated until it becomes ... intolerable.

The word "intolerable" takes us back to the minefield of value judgments and ethics we started with. However, movements such as Spain's anti-austerity "Indignados" and the US "Occupy Wall Street," with its slogan "We are the 99%," are the expression of revolt against an inequality that has become intolerable. They signaled a break in the social compact about what is tolerable and not tolerable, and between the nonaffluent society as a whole and the political and economic elites. This divide is still resolutely in place. The current economic stagnation and surging inequality of the last four decades have invalidated a system empowered by enlargement of the pie and by overall good opportunities and lifestyle conditions, a system only moderately unbalanced. Poverty and social immobility have put an end to that era.

The last decade also shows that this intolerable inequality is associated with a new form of capitalism. Twentieth-century capitalism has evolved into a more aggressive business model, a "deregulated super-capitalism" governed by perverse mechanisms that have produced "too much capitalism" for society.[43] Different tags – Reich's "supercapitalism," Glyn's "unleashed capitalism," Stiglitz's "ersatz capitalism," even Luttwak's "turbo-capitalism" – have been coined to evoke something "designed to create inequalities," in Stiglitz's words.[44] A postcapitalism, we might call it, which goes arm in arm with postdemocracy: a democracy that does not have any supportive normative theory for its capitalism.[45] As Claus Offe has written, it happens now that "the economic resources do determine the agenda of the political process while the owners of those resources themselves ... are not being significantly constrained by social rights and political interventions: markets set the agenda and fiscal constraints of public policies but there is little that public policies can do in terms of constraining the market."[46]

Together with the analysis of the unbalanced relationship between unregulated global markets, growing inequality, and weakening democracy discussed in this chapter, social scientists, pundits, and researchers are also starting to discuss what can be done in order to stop and possibly reverse this social, economic, and political crisis. The next chapter offers a bird's-eye view of some of the main debates.

SIX

The Future of Inequality

> To criticize inequality and to desire equality is not, as is sometimes suggested, to cherish the romantic illusion that men are equal in character and intelligence. It is to hold that, while their natural endowments differ profoundly, it is the mark of a civilized society to aim at eliminating such inequalities as have their source, not in individual differences, but in its own organization, and that individual differences, which are a source of social energy, are more likely to ripen and find expression if social inequalities are, as far as practical, diminished.
>
> Richard H. Tawney, *Equality*

The British economic historian and Christian progressive activist Richard H. Tawney, writing in 1931, had little patience for romantic egalitarianism that refused to acknowledge individual differences. But he also forcefully highlighted the role of institutions in spreading or curbing inequality. Tawney also noticed that a major obstacle to the progress of equality was "the habit of mind" of people adverse to change and accustomed to living in rigidly stratified societies – people, he wrote, who felt "distrust and apprehension for attempts to diminish … sharp differences of economic status, of environment, of education and culture and habit of life."[1]

Tawney's analysis summarizes many important points we have explored in this book. First, inequality, though present in nature, is not inevitable in human societies. Second, values, ideologies, and institutions play a fundamental role in how and to what extent a society adopts policies that curb inequality. Third, excessive inequality is socially disruptive and lowers the standard of living of all members of a community, including the well-off. Fourth, policies are needed to redress inequality.

The last point in particular is the subject of this chapter. The market alone is unable to address complex social issues such as inequality. Laissez-faire in the sense of deregulation, in other words, is a false and ultimately inefficient myth. We need effective policies that reverse current mechanisms of increasing marginalization and on which a newly inclusive social compact can be solidly founded.

As we saw in chapter 1, even though nobody denies the reality of inequality, not all consider it of relevance. Some, for example, claim that poverty, not inequality, is the issue. At the policy level, however, the supporters of these at times opposing views not infrequently end up focusing on the same policies, for the simple reason that high levels of inequality are often accompanied by extreme poverty. Thus, supporters of poverty-biased and inequality-biased policies, while perhaps philosophically and politically distant, may turn out to be fellow travelers.

Reassuringly, nobody – not even those who consider inequality the wrong issue – today sings the beauty of inequality, as was customary only a little more than a century ago. For example, four-time British prime minister William E. Gladstone – who, because of his liberal and reformist positions, was known as "the People's William" – openly spoke of the "love of inequality" as a fundamental element of British civilization: "Call this love of inequality by what name you please – the complement of the love of freedom, or its negative pole, or the shadow which the love of freedom casts, or the reverberation of its voice in the halls of the constitution – it is an active, living, and life-giving power, which forms an inseparable essential element in our political habits of mind, and asserts itself at every step in the processes of our system."[2]

What has died as a creed, however, may survive as habit, and inequality is no exception. Policies to overcome or limit it are thus an essential part of any discussion of inequality itself. Our goal is to provide the reader with a map of some of the most important policy issues debated by scholars, pundits, and politicians who consider inequality a major problem of modern societies.

Recent political developments in many countries, such as the election of Donald Trump as the president of the United States on an isolationist and protectionist political platform and the decision of the United Kingdom to leave the European Union on a more ambiguous agenda (a "global Britain," in the words of Prime Minister Theresa May, yet isolationist with respect to Europe), will undoubtedly give a new spin to these issues. Irrespective of whether one considers these backward-looking visions of a renewed national greatness based on isolationist preeminence self-delusional or actually effective, inequality will remain a fundamental problem to be addressed. The discussion below provides a basic orientation to the issues at stake.

In previous chapters, we raised the separate concepts of within-country and between-country inequality. Here we adopt the same distinction, although obviously, linkages between the two kinds of inequality are deep and important. In a globalized world, such as the one we live in, it could not be otherwise.

WITHIN-COUNTRY INEQUALITY

Inequality is first perceived within the borders of a national community. Depending on the social structure of the society under consideration, scholars and pundits usually propose different sets of policies. For the sake of the argument we will consider only two groups of countries, the economically advanced countries and the less developed ones. Obviously, this partition cannot do justice to the many different conditions of less advanced countries, but space does not allow us to be more nuanced.

Within-Country Inequality in Advanced Economies

The growing difficulties of the welfare state and the representative crisis of many advanced social democracies have brought inequality to the top of the political agenda. The novelty of the last few years is that inequality, in other words, has been recognized as an urgent problem not only of remote and less developed peripheral countries but of industrialized countries at the core of the democratic and capitalist world. The discussion has focused on a number of policies. Not unexpectedly, fiscal policies figure chief among them.

Fiscal Policies

In the last five decades, many countries have witnessed huge decreases in the tax rate of top income brackets. The promise of "cutting taxes" for all citizens indiscriminately, even though it actually benefits almost exclusively those who do not need it, has become a powerful message in the political arena.

According to Thomas Piketty, however, a fundamental historical law is that the rate of return on "capital" (Piketty's word for the market value of total wealth, from financial assets to land and housing) is higher than the rate of growth of the economy. Except for relatively short and specific periods such as wars, when gains are curbed and wealth is both mobilized for the war effort and destroyed, "capitalists" become increasingly richer than the rest of the population, and inequality is constantly on the rise. Piketty's proposal to reduce inequality among members of the national community is thus to greatly *increase* the progressivity of the fiscal system so that the highest tax brackets would reach a tax rate of approximately 80 per cent. Obviously, this would require a high degree of international coordination, as otherwise capitalists would simply move to a more wealth-friendly country.[3] Even though Piketty's historical and economic analysis has been criticized from a broad spectrum of scholars, here the point is that a greater progressivity of the fiscal system is a well-established mechanism to moderate inegalitarian forces.[4] As such, it has been proposed by a number of economists, along with other fiscal reforms, such as a cut on consumption taxes like the value-added tax, which, imposing the same tax on all, irrespective of their income, is highly regressive.

A second point is that historical record shows that fiscal progressivity can go hand in hand with economic growth. In the United States, for example, during the thirty glorious years of rapid economic growth following the Second World War, the top federal income tax rate never fell below 70 per cent (the Nixon and Ford administrations).

With regard to this issue, it is worth mentioning that the opposition to fiscal progressivity is highly ideological. President Barack Obama was accused of being a socialist for having raised the top federal income tax rate from 35 per cent (which he inherited from the George W. Bush administration) to 39.6 per cent in his second mandate. President Ronald Reagan, the lighthouse of modern conservatism, kept the top federal income tax rate at 50 per cent for five consecutive years (1982–86; in 1981 it was 69 per cent). During the ten years of the Republican and Democratic administrations of Dwight D. Eisenhower and John F. Kennedy (1953–63, a decade of remarkable economic growth and low inequality), the top federal income tax rate remained at the staggering level of 91 per cent (with one exception, during Eisenhower's first year, when it was 92 per cent). In addition to tax rates, tax brackets and their thresholds are equally important. For instance, to evaluate the actual progressivity of a fiscal system, we need to know the income threshold at which the top rate applies. Historically, this has considerably changed. During the Eisenhower and Kennedy years, the top federal bracket included incomes higher than \$3.5 million and \$3.1 million (in 2016 US dollars), respectively; higher than \$1.2 million during the Nixon administration; higher than a threshold fluctuating between \$250,000 and \$190,000 during the Reagan administration; and higher than \$400,000 during the Obama administration.[5]

Corporate Institutional Reforms

There are also other ways to limit inequality and invert its trend. They are not alternative but complementary to fiscal policies. Institutional reforms in the financial and corporate world, for example, are strongly needed. On one side, they should aim at curbing excessive risk-taking behaviors and CEOs' unaccountability and self-interested management decisions. Also, they should increase the transparency of financial operations. The taxation of short-term speculative transactions on foreign exchange markets, as proposed in 1972 by the Nobel laureate James Tobin (later expanded to other types of speculative financial transactions and commonly known as the Tobin tax), has also been proposed as a way to penalize speculation.[6] On the other side, policies to reduce the increasingly unfettered power of firms and corporations should be put in place, such as antitrust programs and higher minimum wage legislation. Policies in support of increasing unionization and collective and national wage bargaining, widely accepted between the 1950s and the early 1980s, are today much more contentious, even on the center-left of the political spectrum.

Last but not least, the broadening and universalization of social security systems is a fundamental step toward reducing inequality.[7] Not by chance, the United States is both the only advanced country without a universal and mandatory health insurance system and the advanced country with the highest inequality as measured by the Gini coefficient.

Anthony Atkinson persuasively summarized many of these issues in a September 2016 interview in which he emphasized not only the interconnectedness of inequality policies on many fronts but also the need to rethink our vision of the social compact. Atkinson denounced the ideological insufficiency of the narrowly self-interested individualism that emerged in the last three decades or so, arguing instead that corporate institutions should recuperate the "broader view of their responsibilities" that they used to have in the past, when "they recognised that they had a responsibility in addition to that to their shareholders – also to their workers and to their consumers."[8] Furthermore, Atkinson underscored the crucial role that governments retain (even in a globalized era characterized by a number of transnational or supranational phenomena) by "giving priorities about what kind of technology we'd like to see in what areas, which industries, which activities," thus working in the interest of all social actors and individuals, not only corporate interests.[9]

Educational Policies

The role of government is also eloquently represented by how it can affect what Nobel laureate Jan Tinbergen once described as the "'race' between technical progress and ... third-level education" (or, in more recent parlance, the race between education and technology).[10] Briefly put, technological progress is, according to a broad consensus, skill-biased, in the sense that it requires increasingly skilled labourers. Investment in human capital is thus a fundamental equalizing force insofar as it enables individuals to access high-quality education and keep up with the pace of increasingly skill-biased technology. A poor educational system, on the other hand, makes the supply of human capital lag behind technological progress, thus widening the income gap between those who can take advantage of a first-rate higher education and those who cannot get access to it. As Claudia Goldin and Lawrence F. Katz have shown, while the "college premium" fell from 1915 to 1980, thus narrowing wage differentials, at the turn of the twenty-first century both inequality and the pecuniary return on education had risen again to the high levels of one century earlier.[11]

College attendance and educational attainment are considered important factors in explaining inequality dynamics. The economists David Card and John DiNardo, however, have noticed the lack of synchronicity between the peak of increasing income inequality (which, they say, occurred in the late 1980s) and the major acceleration in technological change (which, as measured by computer use, occurred in the 1990s) or, perhaps even more puzzling, the fall in the relative remuneration of computer science and engineering graduates compared to that of other professionals. James Galbraith has repeatedly underscored the lack of solid data foundations for the skill-biased thesis, first in his 1998 *Created Unequal* and later in his 2012 *Inequality and*

Instability.[12] Some analysts have highlighted other puzzling phenomena that do not easily fit with the skill-biased technological change explanation, such as the fact that an increasing number of college graduates now accept jobs that were previously done by people without a college degree. This reveals an excess supply of skilled labour. Although employed, these college graduates are in fact *overqualified* for the job market. Finally, other causes of increasing wage inequality have more to do with regulatory policies of the job market and with trade policies than with the relationship between education and technology, such as the very low level of the minimum wage, policies that discourage the organization of workers into unions, and the relocation abroad of manufacturing jobs.[13]

In any case, the increasing gap in educational achievement produces important self-reinforcing mechanisms that propagate to other spheres of social inequality. Different levels of education are also a measure of class and other manifestations of social stratification. As the social scientist Heather Beth Johnson has convincingly argued, for example, in the United States, economic inequality is strongly correlated with race inequality. Not unexpectedly, this double-dimensional inequality affects both access to education and the quality of education to which different groups of individuals can get access, eventually perpetuating and even increasing the racial gap. And yet education is, ironically, among the strongest foundations of the American myth of meritocracy. As Johnson puts it, "Education is the institution that is supposed to perform the 'great equalizer' task in our society; where, regardless of background, all children will be given equal opportunity for success based on their individual achievement and merit."[14] With inequality on the rise, this is increasingly less the case. In addition, as Samuel Bowles, Steven N. Durlauf, and Karla Hoff note, increasing inequality in income, education, wealth, and power has repercussions for support (or lack thereof) for public schools, public goods, and so on, thereby creating powerful inequality and poverty traps.[15]

Inequality and Social Mobility

There is no doubt, in sum, that the inequality issue is a political question par excellence, even when we enter the apparently technocratic territories of technological progress and the future of high-quality education. Overall productivity increases have not benefited the middle and lower-middle classes of advanced countries but only those at the top of the earnings pyramid. In fact, the incomes of the middle class in advanced economies have been stagnating for forty years. As Melissa Schettini Kearney has noted, between 1947 and 1975 families at the bottom and the top of the income distribution shared the fruits of strong economic growth, almost doubling their incomes in less than thirty years. Between 1975 and 2010, however, families in the bottom 20 per cent saw an income gain of less than 4 per cent, while families in the top 5 per cent experienced a gain of almost 60 per cent. Like Goldin and Katz, Schettini Kearney also considers this increasing inequality to be the result of technological progress that has favored the "very highly skilled."[16] Moreover, Schettini Kearney also underscores the connection between rising inequality and increasing educational gaps between rich and poor families.[17] These increasing gaps threaten to exacerbate inequality between generations, and thus reduce social mobility. Inequality of incomes, in other words, passes from one generation to the next, and greater inequality in one generation results in greater inequality in the next generation.[18] In sum, as we also note in chapter 5, the higher the inequality in a society, the lower is the intergenerational mobility.

As one who has lived the American dream to the highest degree, former President Barack Obama has underscored the political dimension undergirding the problem of increasing inequality. "People's frustration," he said at a gathering on economic mobility, "is rooted in the nagging sense that no matter how hard they work, the deck is stacked against them. And it's rooted in the fear that their kids won't be better off than they were." Political choices can address or ignore this frustration, and in both cases they will have lasting effects. As Obama put it, "The combined trends of increased inequality and decreasing mobility pose a fundamental threat to the American Dream."[19] And at least in this case, what is true for the United States is true for the world.

Within-Country Inequality in Less Developed Economies

The discussion about less developed countries touches on many of the issues discussed above with regard to advanced economies. Although in many cases these issues are treated somewhat differently when less developed countries are concerned, their major characteristics are similar enough for us not to repeat ourselves. For example, trends in the remuneration of capital and highly skilled labour are a global phenomenon that affects both developed and less developed countries. At the same time, however, emerging economies have been able to compete with certain sectors of advanced economies thanks to their own cheaper labour costs. Although support for education and the training of skilled labour is thus important for all countries, specific short- and medium-term industrial policies, for example, may differ from one country to the other.

An important theme is the institutional framework of

modern-day economies, developed and less developed alike. Economic, social, and institutional reforms are often badly needed in less developed countries. As scholars such as Dani Rodrik and Joseph Stiglitz have convincingly demonstrated, however, shock therapy has almost invariably proved disastrous. Gradualist and selective reforms, consensus building, the creation of an institutional infrastructure (which cannot happen overnight), phased restructuring, room for policy latitude – in sum, a sensitivity to the dynamics of change and transition – are equally as important if not more important. In Stiglitz's words, "successful economic programs require extreme care in *sequencing* – the order in which reforms occur – and pacing."[20] Dani Rodrik also insists on contextual reform, sequencing, and selectivity.

Other questions that affect inequality dynamics and structure in broader terms, however, are specific to the reality of less developed countries, and they deserve a mention. A long sociological tradition has underscored important characteristics of premodern societies, such as very limited, if not nonexistent, social mobility; the preeminence of personal bonds within a community framework over impersonal relations; the absence of – or the deep limitations to – the rule of law; the prevalence of rent-seeking over entrepreneurial behaviors, and so on. The more recent economics literature has rediscovered the importance of some of these themes with the analysis of "limited access" societies and "extracting institutions" as major causes of the inability of these societies to evolve into modern liberal democracies.[21] Again with much simplification (and a lack of historical sensitivity, as we must not forget how early twentieth-century democracies turned into totalitarian and corporatist regimes), modern democracies have usually been considered the place of social mobility, political compromise, and economic redistribution.

This "neo-institutionalist" literature focuses on how less developed countries can evolve in such a way that elites who have positioned themselves as gatekeepers of the economic and political resources of their societies accept the inclusion of increasingly larger strata of the population in a democratic process governing growing access to, and redistribution of, these resources. A number of poor countries, especially in sub-Saharan Africa, whose economy rests on the exploitation of natural resources are good cases in point. Even when international terms of trade are favorable and the economies of these countries grow faster than those of more advanced countries, the revenues from natural resources are usually monopolized by small and self-contained elites, with no benefit for the rest of the population. In these cases, inequality will probably be on the rise despite a country's positive economic performance.[22] From a within-country perspective, the task will therefore be to strengthen a country's democratic institutions and redistributive policies. Critics of neo-institutionalist economics literature notice that, in the end, this is only a restatement of conventional free-market theory. Its point, in other words, seems to be how to introduce Western-style market-oriented institutions in less developed countries, paying only lip service to social institutions and the economic role of governments. Jeff Madrick, for example, has noted that Acemoglu and Robinson's 500-page book mentions trade unions only five times and minimum wage twice. Also, the book never mentions policies such as the protection of infant industries, even though such policies were in fact implemented throughout most of America's history.[23]

A solution to this controversy and, more generally, to how institutions can be modified in favor of increasing redistribution and growth goes beyond the limits of this book. But it is worth noticing that the complexity and context specificity of these processes require deep and sophisticated analysis. To take just one notable example, the World Bank, for decades considered a major proselytizer of one-size-fits-all policies and of the virtues of applying long lists of macroeconomic reforms to very different contexts, more recently has turned to deep historical analysis to understand the process of institutional change.[24]

BETWEEN-COUNTRY INEQUALITY

Growth has been one of the most important issues in the social sciences of the last three centuries. And yet, as the current predicament of the developed world shows, growth is not sufficient to address the inequality issue. Of course, if a country experiences a high rate of growth, its citizens will probably (though not necessarily) better their own position in the global income distribution. More specifically, in an international perspective, the reduction of inequality has to do with how less developed countries can join the "convergence club." From an actually "global" perspective – a perspective, in other words, that considers not the average GDP per capita of national communities but the actual income of individual citizens in the global distribution – the question is more complicated, as it has to do with both domestic redistributive forces and the economic growth of a country in the global scenario.

We should be clear on one point, however. Although growth is not per se sufficient, it remains a necessary element not only for reducing national poverties but also for redressing international and global inequality, at least in the current globalizing age. There exists a vast consensus among inequality scholars and economists from many disparate traditions according to which economic growth is the most powerful tool for reducing poverty and inequality.[25] The current wave of globalization has deeply influenced the ways in which inequality has taken shape nationally and at the global level. First, by lowering the compensation for unskilled work and increasing instead the remuneration of capital and highly skilled work, globalization has polarized within-country income distributions. Second, by increasing economic interconnections and unfettering international markets, it has heightened global competition.[26] While some regions, such as China and other Southeast Asian countries, are successfully riding the globalization wave and catching up with the most advanced countries, other regions are increasingly lagging behind, most prominently Africa. The emergence of populous countries experiencing high rates of economic growth has contributed to shaping the consensus that, if within-country inequality is on the rise, between-country inequality, on the contrary, is decreasing. In this analysis, China (up to 2000) and China and India (since the 2000s) are the "great stabilizers" of global inequality.

And yet two comments are in order. The first and less important one is that, at a certain point, the growth of China and then other populous countries will start to have an adverse effect on global inequality. This will happen when China's standard of living, for example, grows above the threshold of the world average, or, in other words, when the positive effect of reducing the distance from advanced countries will no longer suffice to outweigh the negative effect of increasing the distance from stagnating countries. It will not happen soon, although it will probably happen at some point. This is not, however, an urgent matter. Let's consider it a reminder that apparently positive and unchanging dynamics may actually develop adverse effects at a certain level of their apparently regular evolution.

The second point is both more pressing and more important, namely, that the world is not made up solely of "advanced" and "emerging" (or "catching-up") economies but also of large areas that are increasingly left behind and that remain at the bottom of the international economic pyramid. Africa is by far the most prominent example. Since the process of decolonization and attempts at economic reforms and diversification between the 1950s and 1960s, many African countries have experienced very disappointing economic results. Whereas the 1960s were dubbed "the development decade," the 1980s are remembered as "the lost decade" for all developing countries, and for African countries in particular. The sparse growth that has taken place since then has been more the result of an increase in the international prices of raw materials than of autonomous processes of economic growth. Because the terms of trade of raw materials tend to fluctuate, they cannot be taken as a solid base for a process of catching up, especially on a continent whose population is expected to increase significantly in the next thirty years or so. According to current projections, by 2050 sub-Saharan Africa will account for more than 20 per cent of the world's population. Economic growth is thus, for Africa, desperately important. This brings us back to our earlier discussion of the need for policies that curb within-country inequality and foster a process of autonomous growth not based solely on the export of primary products.

With regard to international economic relations, it is important to note that Africa's growth in the 1980s and the 1990s was severely sabotaged by ill-conceived structural adjustment policies imposed on it by rich countries. Africa's stagnation, in turn, is at the root of a global phenomenon that has become dramatically conspicuous in the last few years, that is, international migrations (with which we opened chapter 4).

Long-term migratory trends are the outcome of decades-long economic stagnation and oppressive regimes, many of which were in place well before the current crisis in Northern Africa and the Middle East erupted. The relatively recent development of global media and communications systems, moreover, helped ease these population flows in many ways. For example, modern communications have made differences in the standard of living more glaringly visible. Also, the diffusion of mobile telephones has helped those who left maintain contact with those who stayed behind, thus strengthening migratory chains. It is the increasing poverty and destitution of the countries of origin, however, that (in addition to crises dictated by wars) is the main long-term cause of international migrations.

Undoubtedly, for those who succeed, migration is the best way to boost their personal income and move up in the global income distribution. We are not speaking here of highly skilled migrants who move from one rich country to another rich country to take advantage of job opportunities, in possession of a regular work visa and a comfortable seat on an airplane. Gains in global income distribution accrue also to individuals who migrate without immigration and job permits, who do not know the language of the country of destination, who are often unskilled, and who end up in poorly remunerated jobs. Moreover, this is true not only at the individual level but, at least up to a certain extent, also at the community level, because of the positive feedbacks that migration triggers both in countries of origin and in countries of destination. And yet strong migratory flows produce a number of interconnected social and economic effects that must be seriously considered to avoid further impoverishing countries of origin or creating explosive situations in countries of destination.[27] The effects of international migrations are not univocally positive, and unrestrained migrations, as Joseph Stiglitz puts it, "may result in a lowering of the welfare of both the country receiving the migrants *and* the country sending them. Even when the country as a whole benefits, there may be great distributive consequences, with large segments of the population – even a majority – worse off. The only sure winners are the migrants themselves and the corporations that get their cheaper labour."[28]

Dealing with migratory flows involves not only multilateral coordination, though this is badly needed. As Milanovic rightly notes, international migrations are one of the few global phenomena that are not the focus of specific multilateral policy action; in contrast, multilateral institutions exist for the governance of economic development, international debt, trade, health, and central banking.[29] First and foremost, a structural reduction in migratory flows requires the fostering of economic growth and opportunities in the countries of origin. Once again, we return to the question of how to promote within-country self-sustaining economic growth and develop fairer international trade. These issues alone are the subject of entire libraries, but we can mention a couple of aspects that have to do with global inequality.

First, international aid from rich countries to poor countries is an almost dry creek of resources, averaging only 0.35 per cent of the GDP of advanced economies. Since the late 1960s, rich countries have been discussing the goal of devoting 0.7 per cent of their gross national income to foreign aid, but except for a few Scandinavian countries, they have never reached this admittedly achievable goal. In comparison, remittances from migrants to their families in the countries of origin constitute a much higher flow. If official development aid is about $130 billion, remittances from rich to less developed countries total approximately $400 billion. In percentage terms, remittances account on average for 6 per cent of the economies of the countries of origin.[30] Furthermore, rich countries pose a number of restrictions on trade with less developed countries that are particularly odious insofar as they make it more difficult for less developed countries, and especially for African countries, to get access to large markets – and thus develop production – of manufactured goods, which are less prone to oscillations in the terms of trade than agricultural produce is.

Analysts such as Jeffrey Sachs of Columbia University have repeatedly claimed that despite all the limitations of international aid policies, the shallow stream of resources should grow to much higher volumes. If underdevelopment is still a problem, this is because not enough resources have been devoted to fight it once and for all.[31] Although one must be particularly careful with this kind of generalization, a huge number of scholars have documented the positive effect of aid on economic growth. Camelia Minoiu and Sanjay G. Reddy, in particular, have studied how developmental aid, if apparently ineffective in the short run, is able to make a difference in the long run.[32]

Others, however, are much more dubious about aid effectiveness. Noticing that in the last decades, aid to Africa has constantly increased, while growth was actually decreasing, the Nobel laureate Angus Deaton has called foreign aid a "resounding failure."[33] According to Deaton and other scholars, such as the New York University economist William Easterly, foreign aid faces an inescapable dilemma, as aid is either useless, when local conditions are hostile to development, or not required, when local conditions are already favorable. "Experts" are often out of touch with the needs and realities of the country they are supposed to help. In place of increasing flows of financial resources (what Deaton mockingly calls the "hydraulic" approach to foreign aid), Deaton urges advanced countries to act at a distance, to focus on small-scale aid, to emphasize the role of technical advice versus financial aid, and, last but not least, to enforce a real moratorium on arms sales to less developed countries.[34]

Finally, the economic growth of the less-developed world, in addition to that of the highly populous emerging countries, will make the issue of ecologically sustainable development even more serious in the future than it is today. From the perspective of a global redistribution of income, this implies that the rich world should take the largest part of the necessary readjustment to make growth ecologically sustainable.

These are all difficult questions, often politically highly charged. As is evident from the political debates of recent years, it is not easy for national communities to address the problem of inequality dispassionately and at the same time empathically. If we broaden our horizon beyond the national borders, we witness the feeling of social cohesion and shared citizenship plummet. To take a dismal example, the European Union redistributes less than 1 per cent of the European income among member countries, since many countries of the EU – chief among them its strongest economy, Germany – refuse to consider it a transfer union, that is, a union in which, because of shared values of solidarity and social cohesion *at the continental level*, countries in a strong position transfer resources to those in need. As mentioned, the official aid from rich to poor countries amounts to a minuscule figure.

Reducing inequality at every level will require deep and continuous action for political reform, especially when reformist action is challenged by much more powerful and often worrisome populist and extremist movements. The hope for and vision of a better world are fundamental ingredients for successful policy action.

APPENDIX

Measures of Inequality

> Some of the things we care the most about are the most difficult to measure, and conversely, the things we find it easiest to measure are sometimes those about which we have relatively little reason to care.
>
> James K. Galbraith, *Inequality*

As the discussion in this book has made amply clear, not only is economic inequality a contentious issue and a multifaceted concept, the statistical work that undergirds inequality studies is complex and ever evolving. The chapters of this book have discussed inequality without delving excessively into technicalities. This appendix offers additional information on some of the most relevant statistical concepts. Even for nonstatisticians, it is important to be conversant with these concepts.[1]

INCOME

Income and other purely economic concepts offer an incomplete and somewhat distorted representation of the actual well-being of a person or a group. This is neither a new nor a radical statement. A commission that included several Nobel laureates in economics, for example, recently highlighted how a macroeconomic indicator as pervasive as the gross domestic product (GDP) per capita is totally inadequate to capture the well-being of a society and its individuals, or to explore fundamental issues such as sustainability, not to mention resource distribution.[2]

At the same time, creating new indices and changing existing ones poses a number of statistical and analytical problems that make the search for better measures far from a banal and easy endeavor. At the national level, for example, the inadequacy of aggregate income to gauge the well-being of individuals has prompted the elaboration of the Human Development Index (HDI), which complements per capita income information with data on life expectancy and education.[3] First presented by the United Nations Development Program in 1990, the HDI embodies the increasing awareness that whereas economic resources are a necessary element for the well-being of individuals, they are by no means sufficient.

Though aware of the limits of measures such as those based exclusively on income, inequality scholars have nonetheless adopted them as their standard reference.[4] There are good reasons for this choice. In their attempts to elaborate increasingly detailed analyses of national and global inequality, they face problems of comparability that make the focus on a single economic indicator necessary. The assumption, as Angus Deaton and Salman Zaidi put it, is that this single economic indicator can be considered a reasonable "summary measure of living standards, itself an important component of human welfare."[5]

Income is a composite quantity that includes wages, salaries, profits, and rents. This is known as the *market income*. If we add social transfers such as government-provided pensions and unemployment subsidies, and deduct taxes from the market income figure, we obtain the *disposable income.*

Disposable income is the base figure that inequality scholars prefer because it takes into account a number of variables that affect the well-being of a person. Disposable income is used whenever actual data about household incomes are available, that is, primarily in calculations that take within-country distributions into account, but also, as we will see below, in a specific approach to calculating inequality at the global level.

THREE DIFFERENT CONCEPTS OF INTERNATIONAL INEQUALITY

For international comparisons, inequality scholars often rely on aggregate data from national accounts, and more specifically on variables such as a country's GDP. The GDP is the total value of goods and services produced for final demand in a territory (usually a country or a region) in a certain period (usually one year) or, alternatively, the sum of monetary consumption, investments, government expenditures, and net exports (exports less imports) that have taken place in a territory within a certain period, or else as the sum of the incomes of all subjects producing goods and services in a country in a specific time period.[6]

Obviously, in international comparisons we are less interested in comparing countries and their absolute GDPs than in comparing the income of their respective populations, that is, the GDP of each country divided by the country's population. This is called *per capita GDP*. For example, whereas we know that the United States is much richer than, say, Singapore, in per capita terms the two countries in 2015 were basically at the same level, that is, US $51,486 and US $51,855, respectively (World Bank data, in constant 2010 US dollars; the use of constant dollars helps avoid the fluctuations in value that result from inflation).[7] In absolute terms, the US economy was approximately fifty-eight times larger than the Singaporean economy ($16,550 billion versus $287 billion), yet the US population was also fifty-eight times larger than Singapore's (319 million people versus 5.5 million).[8] The GDP accruing to each citizen in the two countries thus was on average the same. The same kind of comparison with other countries may produce very different results. China, for example, the world's most populous country, being home to almost one-fifth the world's population, with an absolute GDP of US $8,798 billion (much higher than Singapore's yet not as high as that of the United States), had a per capita GDP in 2015 of US $6,416, or eight times lower than that of the United States or Singapore.[9] India, the second most populous county, with 1.3 billion inhabitants and a GDP of US $2,367 billion (in constant 2010 US dollars), in 2015 had a GDP per capita of US $1,805, or twenty-eight times lower than that of the United States and Singapore and less than one-third China's per capita GDP.

When we discuss international economic inequality, the economic dimension of a country, as represented by the country's GDP, is clearly an important element of the picture but by no means a sufficient one. The size of the population too is a crucial variable since it is the denominator of the ratio GDP/population from which the per capita GDP is derived.

The concept of international inequality introduced here, based on a comparison of the GDP per capita of different countries, offers valuable information. Yet in some important respects it remains very rudimentary. For instance, it could be argued that it heavily distorts our ability to gauge changes in international inequality as it does not consider how populous one country is in absolute terms. India and Nicaragua, for example, in 2015 had a very similar per capita GDP (US $1,806 and US $1,849, in constant 2010 US dollars).[10] Still, it is clear that international inequality would change more drastically if India's per capita GDP increased than if the same increase accrued to Nicaragua's per capita GDP, for the simple reason that in the former case 1.3 billion people would become richer, whereas in the latter case only 6 million would. To take into account this difference, scholars usually calculate *population-weighted* international inequality.

There is no consensus among researchers on what terminology to adopt for these two concepts of inequality. François Bourguignon and Branko Milanovic, for example, two renowned students of inequality and colleagues at the World Bank for many years, use different terms. Whereas Bourguignon calls the unweighted concept "international income scale" and the population-weighted concept "international inequality," Milanovic refers to the first concept as "unweighted international inequality" and to the second concept as "population-weighted international inequality," although he also notes that others call the former "international inequality" and the latter "world inequality."[11] This difference seems to rest on the fact that while international inequality measures inequality between countries, with no consideration for what share of the world population each country hosts on its own territory, world inequality measures inequality among the various populations of the world, defined in national terms. To avoid confusion, Milanovic also proposes to call unweighted international inequality "concept 1 inequality" and world (population-weighted) inequality "concept 2 inequality."

Concept 2 inequality is also an approximation, like concept 1 inequality. It recognizes that different countries have different "magnitudes" on the world stage. Yet, like concept 1 inequality, it describes national populations by way of one single, average, per capita GDP. In other words, concept 2 inequality measures international inequality as if all individuals living in China earned, in 2015, the equivalent of US $6,416, while all individuals living in the United States earned US $51,486. As we know, the world does not work this way, and both in China and in the United States, as in many other countries in the world, we can find extreme poverty and staggering affluence. Concept 2 inequality, in other words, does not consider within-country inequality, as by definition it considers all the individuals living in a certain country as earning the same income.

Some researchers have therefore begun to work with a new and more sophisticated concept of inequality, which they call "global" inequality, to differentiate it from "international" or "world" inequality. Global inequality – or, in Milanovic's terms, concept 3 inequality – takes into account that each country is home to both poor and rich people.[12] From this perspective, working with national averages makes little sense, and these researchers have begun to study inequality among individuals in the world as if everyone belonged to one single country, that is, one country encompassing the entire world. To sum up, global inequality conflates a domestic perspective (within-country inequality) and an international perspective (between-country inequality) to describe in a much more realistic way what is actually happening in global inequality trends.

HOUSEHOLD SURVEYS

Researchers adopting this approach base their calculations on data previously unavailable at the global level, namely, data from household surveys, which are being conducted in an increasing number of countries. In other words, instead of relying on macrodata such as private income and consumption based on GDP calculations, they rely on microdata collected through door-to-door surveys reporting the economic situation of actual households. In this way they can work at a level of detail that was previously unattainable. Of course, surveys do not cover the entire population of a country, but they do provide a sample detailed enough to reflect the variability of incomes within each country. Household surveys in particular are the only sources able to report such individualized, detailed information, and furthermore, they cover the entire distribution from the very poor to the very rich – at least in principle. Data from fiscal sources, for example, don't include data on those who are too poor to pay income taxes and so cover an incomplete population.

Household surveys, however, also present a number of problems: their diffusion to most of the world countries is recent, having taken place in the last thirty to forty years; microdata, especially from old surveys, are not available to researchers; and one often finds discrepancies between microdata and macrodata, making actual data comparisons difficult and prone to error. Moreover, certain groups, especially at either end of the income distribution, are underrepresented. Rich households, for example, tend to underreport their incomes, even though household surveys are anonymous. Also, different institutions use different methods to estimate the standard of living of an individual based on household data: in certain cases this is done simply by dividing the household income by the number of household members, irrespective of their age and the total size of the household. Others prefer to use the concept of "equivalent adult," as the age of the individual members and the total number of members of a household actually affect the household income differently. The Organization for Economic Cooperation and Development, for example, has proposed a widely used equivalence scale: 1 for the first household member, 0.7 for each additional adult, and 0.5 for each child.

The very definition of household income is problematic: in certain cases only income data are collected; in other cases income and consumer spending are both considered. In addition, some surveys consider certain entries, such as virtual income, transfers, or state-offered services, that other surveys exclude from the definition of household income. Some scholars accept the discrepancies as the lesser evil; others apply adjustments (based on national accounts data, which are considered less prone to household survey heterogeneity) to improve consistency and comparability. Obviously, weighing surveys presents its own problems. Finally, whereas some countries conduct broad and frequent surveys, other countries conduct only narrow and infrequent ones, making comparability issues even more relevant.[13]

INTERNATIONAL INCOME COMPARISONS

Another fundamental operation has to do with methods that make sensible international comparisons possible. Does it make sense to compare per capita incomes in the United States and India, converting them into US dollars, as we did above? In fact, what we did was take the GDP of different countries, initially calculated in domestic currency (the US dollar for the United States, the rupee for India, and the Singaporean dollar for Singapore), and convert them all into a common currency, the US dollar (in constant 2010 dollars, that is, dollars of the base year 2010, in order to prevent price inflation from corrupting the calculations). And yet this is not enough.

The conversion to a common currency says very little about the cost of living within specific countries: anyone who has traveled abroad knows that the price of a specific good or service varies from country to country. Converting different currencies into constant US dollars, thus, says nothing about what we can actually buy with those dollars in, say, the United States versus India or Brazil. In fact, if we travel from the United States to India, we will find that many goods and services cost more, in dollar terms, in the United States than in India. This difference is relevant when we want to compare how people actually live on their incomes in their home countries.

To calculate how prices differ among countries, there is no other way but to empirically collect price data in all countries in the world and then compare them. This is done by the International Comparison Project (ICP), managed by the United Nations Statistical Division. From price differences between countries on specific products, ICP statisticians compute price differences on larger categories (such as food), and finally they compute a single average measure that "summarizes" the price difference between countries.[14] The first iteration of the ICP was conducted in 1970 and covered only ten countries. In 1975 it involved thirty-four countries, and thereafter it grew exponentially: in 1985 it involved sixty-four countries, in 2005 146 countries, and in 2011, the last completed round, 199 countries.[15] According to one expert in the field, the ICP is "the single most massive empirical exercise ever conducted in economics."[16] The ICP produces an exchange rate that takes into account the different price levels and consumer structure of each country. In other words, the ICP exchange rates make it possible to compare currencies while maintaining their respective purchasing power unchanged. For this reason, the ICP exchange rates are called purchasing power parity (PPP) exchange rates.

Besides the mere collection of data, the actual statistical work to build PPP exchange rates is complicated and presents some intrinsic problems that make it a far from perfect statistical tool. For example, as one scholar highlights, a major and insoluble problem is the trade-off between the "sameness" of the basket of goods and services that is considered in the comparison across countries and the "representativeness" of this basket. To be strictly comparable, baskets must contain the same list of goods and services. Any given list of goods and services, however, may be more or less representative of consumption and price behaviors depending on which country it is applied to, and so it will capture consumption and price behaviors better in some countries and worse in others. The balance between these two exigencies, between sameness and representativeness, is intrinsically unstable and prone to different interpretations.[17] At its simplest, however, the idea is that if on the international market the Indian rupee to the US dollar exchange rate is 64.15 – in other words, slightly more than 64 rupees will buy one dollar – and the PPP conversion factor calculated by the ICP is 0.3, then in India one does not need 64 rupees to buy the equivalent of what one would buy with one dollar in the United States but only 64.15×0.3, or slightly more than 19 rupees.[18] Clearly, to compare incomes across the world and study inequality trends, we must consider PPP exchange rates, not market ones.

INEQUALITY MEASURES

Finally, scholars calculate inequality levels at the national and international levels. As in the discussion above, our analysis will touch on only the most important concepts.[19] Depending on one's specific interests, it is possible to measure inequality in many different ways.

Positional Indices

One commonly used approach is to compare the incomes of different groups of people. In a 2011 article in *Vanity Fair,* for example, the Nobel laureate Joseph Stiglitz focused on the increasing disparities between the top 1 per cent of income distribution and the rest of the US population.[20] In *The Globalization of Inequality,* François Bourguignon similarly focuses on the share of the national income that goes to the top 1 per cent of the global population, the top 5 per cent, and the top 10 per cent. One can also look at the relative gap between the income of the richest 10 per cent of the global population and the poorest 10 per cent, the so-called P90/P10 ratio.[21] For example, a value of 5 in the P90/P10 ratio means that the income of the poorest person in the top 10 per cent of income distribution is five times that of the richest person in the bottom 10 per cent. Similarly, one could devise yet other ratios according to one's needs, such as the ratio between the median income and the poorest 10 per cent (or the P50/P10 ratio). Such ratios are fairly straightforward and easy to interpret.

These ratios are called positional indices and they offer valuable information about specific questions. The P90/P10 ratio, for example, offers a clear view of the absolute distance in income between the richest and the poorest strata of a population. At the same time, these positional indexes do not say anything about what happens in other parts of the distribution.

José Gabriel Palma of Cambridge University has recently proposed a positional index that seems to offer valuable insight into the inequality trends of several countries around the world. Palma has noted that the share accruing to the middle and upper-middle classes is very similar across countries, irrespective of the specific economic policies those countries adopt. What does change is the share that goes to the richest 10 per cent of the population and to the poorest 40 per cent. Depending on whether we focus on the extremes of the income distribution or on the center of it, Palma writes, "the distributional geometry changes from huge *disparity* to remarkable *similarity*" among countries.[22] In other words, we can observe two opposing forces at work. On one side, the middle and upper-middle classes (which Palma identifies as the individuals who fall between the poorest 50 per cent and the poorest 90 per cent of a population) appropriate an increasingly uniform share of income across nations and world regions. This is a "centripetal" force. On the other side we see a growing bifurcation between the income shares of the richest 10 per cent and the poorest 40 per cent, and this is a "centrifugal" force. Palma argues that the most important thing is to monitor this centrifugal force, and so he proposes to measure inequality by using the ratio between the income share of the richest 10 per cent and the income share of the poorest 40 per cent, since the major shifts in income distribution take place between these two groups. The *Palma ratio*, as this measure has come to be known, has gained a certain popularity in recent years.[23] As James K. Galbraith has recently commented, however, "Whether [the Palma ratio] will go on to become a standard summary measure of inequalities remains to be seen."[24]

The Gini Index

One measure widely used by inequality scholars is the Gini coefficient (researchers use quite interchangeably the terms "Gini coefficient," "Gini index," and "Gini points"). Chapter 3 provides a more in-depth discussion of its historical importance and its relation to other tools in the statistician's tool box. Here we will discuss only a few examples of Gini values with regard to certain countries and its graphic representation, which offers an easy way to grasp what this coefficient means.

The Gini coefficient is characterized by synthesis and simplicity. Despite the complexity of its algebraic calculation, the Gini coefficient lies between the values of 0 (extreme equality) and 1 (extreme inequality). A Gini coefficient of 0.3 thus indicates lower inequality than a coefficient of 0.4. In this way, the value of the Gini coefficient provides us in a single figure with an immediate idea of the level of inequality within a country (and, as a consequence, it makes between-country comparisons possible). For the sake of simplification, the Gini coefficient is often reported on a 0 to 100 scale instead of a 0 to 1 scale. A Gini coefficient of 0.34 on the 0 to 1 scale can thus also be expressed as a Gini coefficient of 34 – or 34 "Gini points" – on the 0 to 100 scale. To take a few examples, the Gini coefficients of Western European countries are often below 30, conventionally indicating low inequality. The Gini values for 2006 (the year preceding the beginning of the recent global crisis, and a year for which we have comparable data on many countries around the world), for example, are 30.6 for Norway, 26.4 for Sweden, 29.3 for Belgium, 25.1 for Denmark, 31.2 for Germany (2005 data), and 28.7 for Austria. These low values are not surprising if we keep in mind the strength and pervasiveness of the welfare state in those countries. Other European countries with higher inequality rates, again not surprisingly, are the United Kingdom (37.2), Italy (33.7), Spain (33.0), and Portugal (38.5). Former Eastern bloc countries present a likewise varied picture. In 2006 the Czech Republic had a Gini value of 26.9 and Bulgaria had a Gini value of 31.0, but Hungary varied from 30 in 2004 to 34.7 in 2006, and Poland has always been in the mid-30s (35.8 in 2006). Central and Latin American countries present a very different situation, with Gini coefficients in the higher 40s or even 50s, such as Peru (49.6), Brazil (53.2), Colombia (58.7), Bolivia (54.2), and Honduras (57.4). Among the economically developed countries, the United States is the only one to surpass the 40.0 threshold. Specifically, in 2006, the Gini coefficient for the United States was 47.0, very close to Uruguay's (47.2) and the Democratic Republic of Congo's (46.9), and more than five points higher than the Russian Federation's, a.k.a. the country of oligarchs (41.6). In the last fifteen years, the most internally equal country seems to have been Azerbaijan, with a Gini coefficient of 17.5 in 2005 (although the figure for 2008 is 31.2), while the most unequal one was South Africa, with a staggering Gini coefficient of 69.8 in 2008 (for the sake of comparison with previous data, it was 67.4 in 2006).[25]

As mentioned, the Gini coefficient is calculated algebraically. Here, however, it may be useful to recall its geometric description, to which Gini himself explicitly refers. This description is based on the Lorenz curve, also discussed in chapter 3. Figure A.1 plots on the horizontal axis the cumulative percentage of the population (households in this case) from poorest to richest – against, on the vertical axis, the cumulative percentage of the total income held by these percentages of the population. With a perfectly egalitarian distribution, the Lorenz curve corresponds to the straight line with an inclination of 45 degrees (the diagonal of the square).

With nonegalitarian distributions, the Lorenz curve bends to the right: a bowed curve shows that a certain x per cent of the population receives less than x per cent of the total income. The more distant this curve is from the 45-degree line – that is, the more bowed it becomes – the greater the inequality is: an increasingly greater percentage of households receives the same percentage of total income, and, consequently, an increasingly

Figure A.1. The Lorenz curve

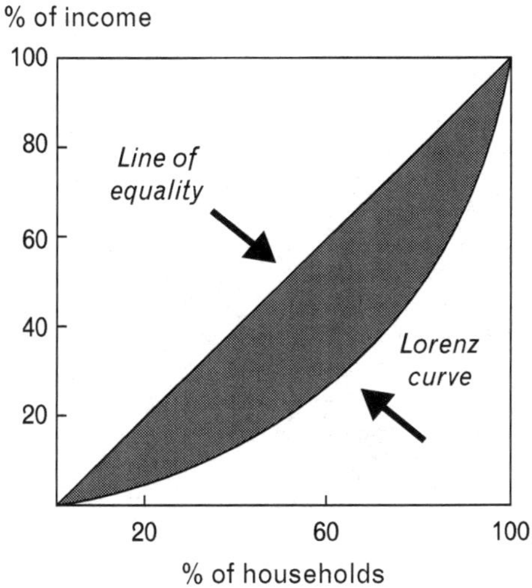

smaller percentage of households receives all the rest (the top 10 per cent, the 1 per cent, the 1 per cent of the 1 per cent, and so on). Thus, if inequality increases as we get farther from the 45-degree straight line, we can easily imagine the Lorenz curve that expresses the highest possible inequality. This will be a curve according to which the entire population except one single individual receives 0 per cent of income, while that one individual receives all the income. This curve will adhere to the horizontal axis, as 99.9 per cent of the population receive 0 income, and then will abruptly move along the vertical axis, corresponding to the one individual receiving the entire income.[26]

The Gini coefficient is the ratio of (1) the area between the Lorenz curve and the 45-degree straight line and (2) the entire

Figure A.2. The Gini coefficient represented through a Lorenz curve

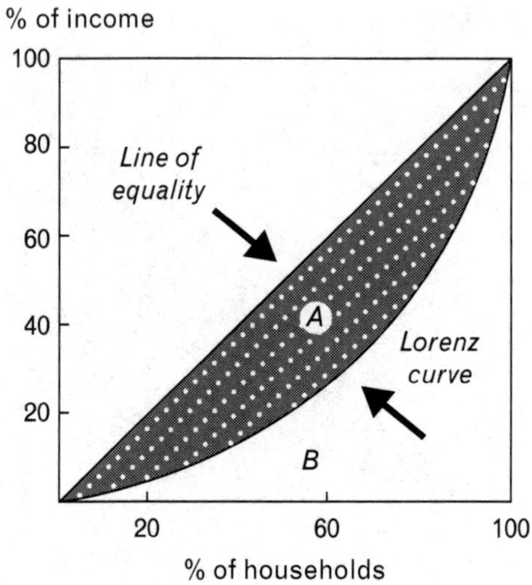

area of the triangle formed by the two axes and the 45-degree straight line (figure A.2). Calling the first area A and the second area $A+B$, the Gini coefficient is:

$$\text{Gini coefficient} = A/(A+B).$$

The extreme values of the Gini coefficient are 0 and 1. And in fact, in the case of perfect equality the Lorenz curve actually adheres to the 45-degree straight line: $A=0$, and the equation resolves to 0. In the opposite case of perfect inequality, the Lorenz curve adheres to the two axes: A covers the entire area of the triangle while B disappears (or its value becomes 0), and thus $A/(A+B)=1$. Interestingly, this geometric representation helps us

Figure A.3. Two Lorenz curves for the same Gini coefficient

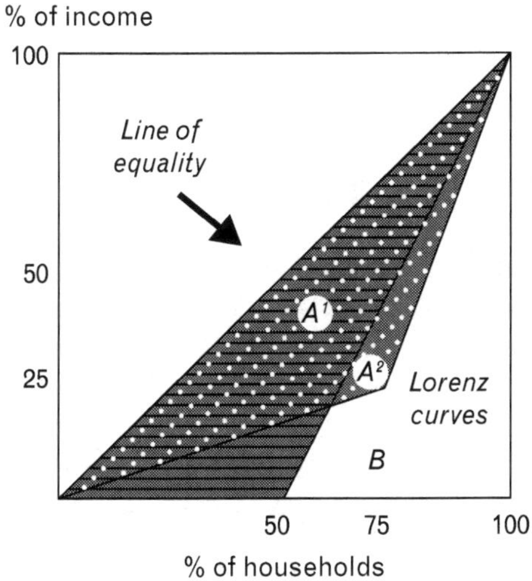

understand one of the main shortcomings of the Gini coefficient mentioned in chapter 3, namely, that very different distributions can have the same Gini value. Let's consider, for instance, a society whose Lorenz curve is straight from (0,0) to (0.5,0) and then straight again from (0.5,0) to (1,1), as in figure A.3. In such a society, half of the population has no income at all, while the other half appropriates the entire income. This society is represented by the area filled with horizontal lines and called A^1. But in another society, in which 75 per cent of population get 25 per cent of the total income and the remaining 25 per cent of population get 75 per cent of income, the Lorenz curve, as depicted in the area filled with white dots and called A^2, is straight from (0,0) to (0.75,0.25) and then straight again from (0.75,0.25) to (1,1).

The two curves are very different, though their Gini coefficient (0,25) is the same.

Theil Statistics

The Gini values we have given above with regard to a number of countries were all based on microdata obtained from household surveys. As mentioned earlier, however, household data are very expensive to obtain, are not always available, and can be compared across different countries and surveys only with great difficulty. To overcome these and other shortcomings of household surveys, James K. Galbraith and his collaborators at the University of Texas decided to focus on industrial pay information. The advantages of working with these data sets are numerous. First, they are commonly used in most countries around the world. Second, they are regularly updated by local administrations (as we have seen, household surveys are irregular and present many problems of cross-country or between-year consistency). Third, they are easily comparable. And finally, because "the inner workings of an economy are highly interdependent" and mutually consistent, it is relatively easy to infer more general conclusions from observations that are often limited in scope.[27] As Galbraith put it, "The part of the economy one observes is (usually, though not always) a window from which the view gives a fair idea of the part one does not see directly."[28] In addition, Galbraith and his group, instead of using the Gini index – which is not exactly decomposable into a between-groups and a within-group component – use the Theil index. This index, as anticipated in chapter 3, has the important characteristic of being decomposable into groups without residual. In other words, given a specific group and its Theil inequality measure, it is possible to obtain the same value of the Theil index as the sum of inequality measures of subsets of that group.

More important, Galbraith and his collaborators noticed that to capture the fundamental inequality dynamics at the national or international level, rather crude levels of aggregation or disaggregation are usually sufficient. What is lost in terms of the refined analysis that only a household survey can offer is gained in terms of comparability among data and groups, regularity and frequency of data availability, and sample coverage. This approach, Galbraith argues, is much less expensive and offers much more possibilities to researchers to group data according to their needs. Most of all, despite its limits and the alleged cruder nature of its data (at least if compared to very fine-grained household surveys), it corresponds reasonably well to other measures, perhaps more sophisticated but weaker in terms of data availability.[29]

INEQUALITY DATABASES

The discussion of Galbraith's alternative approach brings us to another important topic that must be considered when discussing inequality measures, namely, the databases currently available to inequality scholars. The assembly of databases on income distribution dates back to the pioneering work of the United Nations in the 1950s, but until the mid-1970s data collections were still very sparse, incomplete, and only partially comparable. To overcome this bottleneck in the availability and quality of data, in the mid-1990s two World Bank researchers, Klaus Deininger and Lyn Squire, assembled what at the time was the largest possible set of Gini coefficients from the existing literature, putting together more than 2,600 observations (as it relies on previous collections of data, it is considered a "secondary database"). Of these, after further scrutiny, a few less than 700 were, according to Deininger and Squire, "high-quality" observations, as they met three criteria: (1) they were based on household surveys, (2) they offered a full coverage of the population, and (3) they offered a full coverage of the sources of income.

With 682 high-quality observations covering 108 countries, the Deininger-Squire data set became a fundamental reference for inequality scholars. As Deininger and Squire highlighted, their data set had nine times as many observations and three times as many countries covered as the larger data sets previously available.[30] The World Institute for Development Economics Research of the United Nations University extended the Deininger-Squire data set further in the World Income Inequality Database (WIID), first released in 2000 and since then improved with three major updates and a number of minor ones (in January 2017 WIID version 3.4 was published). WIID now collects approximately 8,800 Gini coefficients on 182 countries. The World Bank also absorbed information from the Deininger-Squire data set into a larger database, the World Development Indicators (WDI) database, which includes as well other World Bank and non-World Bank sources.[31]

Because of their secondary nature, however, these databases have also important shortcomings. For example, on closer examination the underlying data appear to rely on different choices of reference unit (household, family, tax unit, or the individual), different concepts of resources utilized (income or expenditure), different comprehensiveness of the definition of income and expenditure (whether income includes or excludes interest and dividends, whether expenditure includes or excludes home production), and so on. The compilers of these databases were aware of these shortcomings but emphasized the importance of building increasingly larger databases. Critical assessments, however, show that internal discrepancies and nonharmonization may give a misleading picture of inequality trends within and between countries. Based on the Deininger-Squire data set, for example, the inequality present in certain countries resulted in grossly overestimated inequality in northern European countries such as Sweden, Denmark, and Norway and underestimated inequality in Spain and Great Britain.[32]

A secondary database that avoids, at least partly, these deficiencies is the OECD Income Distribution Dataset (IDD). Though based on secondary sources, its data are collected through an identical questionnaire that the OECD Statistical Office distributes to national statistical offices or economic departments.[33]

Other research centers have followed a different approach. The Luxembourg Inequality Study (LIS), for example, has consistently focused on collecting microdata from household surveys and making all sources available to researchers. Since pioneering work on ten OECD countries directed by Anthony Atkinson in the early 1990s, the LIS has been considered the gold standard for cross-national comparisons based on microdata. The LIS database, however, is mainly focused on rich countries, and according to some critics the "rich-country bias" of LIS remains a major limitation.[34]

Now housed by the LIS, and before by the World Bank, is the All the Ginis database put together by Branko Milanovic. Originally created in 2004, this database lists more than 2,300 "standardized" Gini coefficients for 166 countries. As with the LIS database, Milanovic's All the Ginis is based without exception on microdata from actual household surveys from nine different sources. The standardization is based on fine-tuning of the different sources, so that more reliable sources for a specific region or period get precedence over less reliable ones. When a conflict among sources arises, the value is excluded from the database. The database, however, is built with all information available, so that researchers can decide to adopt different "precedence" approaches according to their needs. In a sense, the All the Ginis database is a reasoned selection of all Gini values that are of high quality from the best available databases based on microdata. Despite being purely a secondary source, however, this database highly reduces the problems of other secondary databases as it offers a "preferred" set of values (the "Allginis" coefficient) but also leaves the researcher free to use data from one or more source databases.[35]

Another remarkable attempt to harmonize data has been pursued by Frederick Solt at the University of Iowa, who in 2008 published the first version of the Standardized World Income Inequality Database (SWIID). Relying, like Milanovic, on the LIS database and a number of other sources, Solt aimed at overcoming the comparability problems that the All the Ginis database still presented. In its most updated version, SWIID comprises more than 10,000 Gini coefficients for 174 countries, which is, according to its author, "a broader sample of countries and years than any other income inequality data set."[36]

As should by now be clear, inequality data represent a major trade-off between comparability and coverage. The larger the sample of observations, the less comparable are the single data points, as they probably come from different sources with different basic assumptions. High comparability, on the contrary, can be reached if the observations are limited either to a specific source or to a subset of countries surveyed using highly comparable survey methods. The Deininger-Squire and WIID databases resolved the trade-off in favor of coverage. The OECD and LIS databases instead opted for comparability. Milanovic and Solt are trying to walk the difficult line between the two extremes of the trade-off in order to have both large coverage and reasonable comparability.

Two projects that have approached this trade-off in a different way are the University of Texas Inequality Project (UTIP) of James K. Galbraith and his collaborators and the World Top Incomes Database, presented in 2011 and managed by Facundo Alvaredo, Anthony Atkinson, Thomas Piketty, and Emmanuel Saez (WTID, since renamed the World Wealth and Income Database, or WID). Both these efforts conceptualize inequality in a more limited but more consistent way. The UTIP measures differences in average pay between industrial or economic sectors as classified by the United Nations Industrial Development Organization. As Galbraith argues, this approach has the advantage of relying on very common, detailed, harmonized, and inexpensive data.[37] The WID instead measures the share of taxable income as reported on personal tax returns, complemented by other fiscal and survey data, based on the assumption that recent increases in economic inequality have been largely driven by a rise in top incomes and wealth. Obviously, a vast literature highlights in turn the limits of these approaches, but this is not the place to review it.

As this section shows, the efforts to collect, harmonize, and compare data are many and important, and they have hugely increased since the turn of the twenty-first century. This richness of data, however, must be used with judgment, and it is necessary, today more than ever, not to mistake quantity for quality. In a similar fashion, Emmanuel Saez argues that "important gaps remain," and progress in the study of inequality must come "from a combination of data and research."[38] Most of all, as two important scholars of inequality studies and pioneers of data analysis on inequality claim, historical and qualitative analyses remain fundamental: "'Looking at the data' should form part of a narrative approach to economic analysis that combines several different ingredients."[39]

Notes

Introduction

1. See, for example, the focus of Nobel laureate Angus Deaton on economic and health inequality in his *The Great Escape: Health, Wealth, and the Origins of Inequality* (Princeton University Press, 2013).
2. *Income Inequality in the United States: Hearing Before the Joint Economic Committee,* 113th Cong. (2014), 2d Sess. (statement of Robert B. Reich, University of California, Berkeley), January 16.
3. *Opportunity, Mobility, and Inequality in Today's Economy: Hearing Before the Budget Committee, US Senate,* 113th Cong. (2014), 2d Sess. (statement of Joseph E. Stiglitz, Columbia University), April 1.
4. See Peter Scott Campbell, "Democracy v. Concentrated Wealth: In Search of a Louis D. Brandeis Quote," *Green Bag* 16, no. 3 (Spring 2013), pp. 251–56.
5. Alan Greenspan, interview by Daniel Yergin, George Washington University, September 19, 2007.
6. Jonathan D. Ostry, Prakash Loungani, and Davide Furceri, "Neoliberalism: Oversold?," *Finance and Development* (IMF) 53, no. 2 (June 2016), pp. 38–41, at p. 39.
7. See, for example, James K. Galbraith, *Inequality and Instability: A Study of the World Economy Just before the Great Crisis* (Oxford University Press, 2012); Leonardo Gasparini, Guillermo Cruces, and Leopoldo Tornarolli, "Recent Trends in Income Inequality in Latin America,"

Economía 11, no. 2 (Spring 2011), pp. 147–201; and Branko Milanovic, "More or Less," *Finance and Development* (IMF) 48, no. 3 (September 2011), pp. 6–11.

8. Thomas Piketty, *Capital in the Twenty-First Century* (Belknap Press of Harvard University Press, 2014; the original French edition appeared one year earlier); Richard Wilkinson and Kate Pickett, *The Spirit Level: Why Greater Equality Makes Societies Stronger* (London: Allen Lane, 2009); Robert J. Gordon, *The Rise and Fall of American Growth: The US Standard of Living since the Civil War* (Princeton University Press, 2016). For a discussion of Piketty's publishing fortune, see Robert H. Wade, "The Piketty Phenomenon and the Future of Inequality," *Real-World Economics Review* 69 (October 2014), pp. 2–17.
9. Galbraith, *Inequality and Instability*, p. 3.
10. Dani Rodrik, *The Globalization Paradox: Democracy and the Future of the World Economy* (New York: W. W. Norton, 2011).
11. For an insider's perspective on the negotiations between Greece and the troika institutions, see James K. Galbraith, *Welcome to the Poisoned Chalice: The Destruction of Greece and the Future of Europe* (Yale University Press, 2016). On the European crisis, see Joseph E. Stiglitz, *The Euro: How a Common Currency Threatens the Future of Europe* (New York: W. W. Norton, 2016). On the European crisis in historical perspective, see Yanis Varoufakis, *And the Weak Suffer What They Must? Europe, Austerity, and the Threat to Global Stability* (London: Bodley Head, 2016).

1. *Why Inequality Is the Real Issue*

1. Ken Binmore, "The Origins of Fair Play," ELSE Working Paper 267 (London: Centre for Economic Learning and Social Evolution, 2007); Douglass C. North, John J. Wallis, and Barry R. Weingast, *Violence and Social Orders: A Conceptual Framework for Interpreting Recorded Human History* (Cambridge University Press, 2009), p. 31.
2. Angus Deaton, *The Great Escape: Health, Wealth, and the Origins of Inequality* (Princeton University Press, 2013), p. 78. In more philosophical terms, Jean-Jacques Rousseau said something very similar in 1755 when he claimed, "There is hardly any inequality in the state of nature." See Jean-Jacques Rousseau, "A Discourse on a Subject Proposed by the

Academy of Dijon: What is the Origin of Inequality among Men, and is It Authorised by Natural Law?," in *The Social Contract and Discourses*, translated and with an introduction by G. D. H. Cole (London: J. M. Dent, 1923 [1755]), pp. 155–246, at p. 238.

3. Mitt Romney on the *Today Show*, January 11, 2012, as reported in Joseph E. Stiglitz, *The Price of Inequality: How Today's Divided Society Endangers Our Future* (New York: W. W. Norton, 2012), p. 398, note 107.
4. Deirdre N. McCloskey, *Bourgeois Equality: How Ideas, Not Capital or Institutions, Enriched the World* (University of Chicago Press, 2016), p. 47.
5. Ibid., pp. 24 and 46. The share of the bottom 10 per cent is among the most common measures of inequality; we discuss it in chapter 3 and the appendix.
6. Jagdish Bhagwati, *In Defense of Globalization* (Oxford University Press, 2007), p. 67.
7. Harry Frankfurt, "Equality as a Moral Idea," *Ethics* 98, no. 1 (1987), pp. 21–43, at pp. 41, 42, and 23.
8. Albert O. Hirschman, *The Rhetoric of Reaction: Perversity, Futility, Jeopardy* (Belknap Press of Harvard University Press, 1991).
9. Ibid.
10. Branko Milanovic, *The Haves and the Have-Nots: A Brief and Idiosyncratic History of Global Inequality* (New York: Basic Books, 2011), p. 84.
11. At least as an institution, this is the case; several economists who have worked for the World Bank are leading scholars on inequality issues – for example, François Bourguignon, Branko Milanovic, and the Nobel laureate Joseph E. Stiglitz – and yet their scholarly research never became mainstream at the World Bank. For one reason or another, they are now working elsewhere.
12. Robert S. McNamara, "To the Board of Governors, Nairobi, Kenya, September 24, 1973," in *The McNamara Years at the World Bank: Major Policy Addresses of Robert S. McNamara, 1968–1981* (Johns Hopkins University Press, 1981), pp. 242, 258–59.
13. Amartya Sen, *Inequality Reexamined* (Clarendon Press of Oxford University Press, 1992), p. ix, emphasis in the original.
14. Ibid.
15. John Rawls, *A Theory of Justice* (Harvard University Press, 1971).

16. Amartya Sen, "Equality of What?," in *The Tanner Lectures on Human Values,* vol. 1, edited by Sterling M. McMurrin (Cambridge University Press, 1980), pp. 197–220, emphasis added. See also Sen, *Inequality Reexamined.*
17. As explained in Sen, *Inequality Reexamined,* p. xi. For accessible discussions of social justice, see, for example, Amartya K. Sen, "Social Justice and the Distribution of Income," in *Handbook of Income Distribution,* vol. 1, edited by Anthony B. Atkinson and François Bourguignon (Amsterdam: Elsevier, 2000), pp. 59–85; Sophie Elliott, "Why Measure Inequality? A Discussion of the Concept of Equality," *Oxonomics* 4 (2009), pp. 32–40; and Anthony B. Atkinson and Joseph E. Stiglitz, *Lectures on Public Economics,* updated edition (Princeton University Press, 2015).
18. For an introduction to the human development approach, see Martha Nussbaum, *Creating Capabilities: The Human Development Approach* (Harvard University Press, 2010). Deirdre McCloskey, who is a strong advocate of the irrelevance of inequality, still agrees with Sen, Nussbaum, and Stewart on the relevance of achieving "equal sustenance and dignity, eliminating poverty, [and] acquiring for all people what economist Amartya Sen and the philosopher Martha Nussbaum call capabilities" (McCloskey, *Bourgeois Equality,* p. 46).
19. Lawrence Mishel and Josh Bivens, "Occupy Wall Streeters Are Right about Skewed Economic Rewards in the United States," EPI Briefing Paper 331 (Washington: Economic Policy Institute, 2011), p. 6.
20. Raghuram G. Rajan, *Fault Lines: How Hidden Fractures Still Threaten the World Economy* (Princeton University Press, 2010), p. 24.
21. Michael Kumhof and Romain Rancière, "Inequality, Leverage and Crises," IMF Working Paper WP/10/268 (New York: International Monetary Fund, 2010); James K. Galbraith, *Inequality and Instability. A Study of the World Economy Just before the Great Crisis* (Oxford University Press, 2012).
22. Milanovic, *The Haves and the Have-Nots,* pp. 193–94.
23. Rajan, *Fault Lines,* p. 8.
24. Milanovic, *The Haves and the Have-Nots,* p. 195.
25. Kumhof and Rancière explain this causal chain in "Inequality, Leverage and Crises."
26. For example, John Bound and George Johnson, "Changes in the Structure of Wages in the 1980s: An Evaluation of Alternative Explanations,"

American Economic Review 82, no. 3 (1992), pp. 371–92; David H. Autor, Lawrence F. Katz, and Melissa S. Kearney, "The Polarization of the Labor Market," *American Economic Review* 96, no. 2 (May 2006), pp. 189–94; Claudia Goldin and Lawrence F. Katz, *The Race between Education and Technology* (Belknap Press of Harvard University Press, 2010); Melissa S. Kearney, *Income Inequality in the United States: Hearing Before the Joint Economic Committee,* 113th Cong. (2014), 2d Sess., S. Hrg. 113-202 (statement of Melissa Kearney), January 16.

27. Rajan, *Fault Lines.*
28. James K. Galbraith, *Created Unequal: The Crisis in American Pay* (University of Chicago Press, 1998). As Galbraith pointed out in the preface to *Created Unequal* and more recently in his *Inequality and Instability,* the skill-bias view has two comforting political implications for mainstream economic ideology: "It subsume[s] rising inequality into inevitable and desirable technical progress, and it place[s] the onus on individual workers to improve their lot through education and training." As a consequence, it defuses reasons to increase public action on macroeconomic issues (Galbraith, *Inequality and Instability,* p. 125). For a similar view, see Holger Apel, "Income Inequality in the US from 1950 to 2010: The Neglect of the Political," *Real-World Economics Review* 72 (2015), pp. 2–15. See also Anthony B. Atkinson, "The Changing Distribution of Income: Evidence and Explanations," *German Economic Review* 1, no. 1 (2000), pp. 3–18. In relation to OECD countries, see Anthony B. Atkinson, "Income Inequality in OECD Countries: Data and Explanations," *CESifo Economic Studies* 49, no. 4 (2003), pp. 479–513.
29. Gunnar Myrdal, *An American Dilemma* (New York: Harper and Brothers, 1944); Samuel Bowles, Steven N. Durlauf, and Karla Hoff, "Introduction," in *Poverty Traps,* edited by Samuel Bowles, Steven N. Durlauf, and Karla Hoff (New York: Russell Sage Foundation and Princeton University Press, 2006), pp. 1–13; Richard Sennett, *Respect in a World of Inequality* (New York: W. W. Norton, 2003); Samuel Bowles and Herbert Gintis, "The Inheritance of Inequality," *Journal of Economic Perspectives* 16, no. 3 (Summer 2002), pp. 3–30.
30. International Labour Office, *A Fair Globalization: Creating Opportunities for All,* report by the World Commission on the Social Dimension of Globalization (Geneva, 2004), p. x. See also Joseph E. Stiglitz, *Making Globalization Work* (London: Penguin, 2007).

31. Branko Milanovic, "A Short History of Global Inequality: The Past Two Centuries," *Explorations in Economic History* 48, no. 4 (2011), pp. 494–506, at p. 499.
32. On this, see also Thomas Piketty, "Putting Distribution Back at the Center of Economics: Reflections on *Capital in the Twenty-First Century*," *Journal of Economic Perspectives* 29, no. 1 (2015), pp. 67–88.

2. *The Long Neglect of Inequality*

1. This and the following quotations are from Voltaire, *Dictionnaire Philosophique* (Geneva: Gabriel Gasset, 1776), in our translation, based on Theodore Besterman's translation of Voltaire, *Philosophical Dictionary* (London: Penguin, 1972), pp. 181–84.
2. Bronisław Geremek, *Poverty: A History* (Oxford: Blackwell, 1994); Michel Mollat, *Les pauvres au Moyen Âge: Étude sociale* (Paris: Hachette, 1978).
3. Gareth Stedman Jones, *An End to Poverty? A Historical Debate* (Columbia University Press, 2004), p. 8.
4. Roger E. Backhouse, *The Ordinary Business of Life: A History of Economics from the Ancient World to the Twenty-First Century* (Princeton University Press, 2002), p. 132.
5. Marx would probably strongly disagree with being mentioned as a representative of classical political economy for, as Dobb notes, Marx "spoke of the school of classical political economy (a term which he himself originated) as the bourgeois school." See Maurice Dobb, *Theories of Value and Distribution since Adam Smith: Ideology and Economic Theory* (Cambridge University Press, 1973), p. 28.
6. David Ricardo, *Principles of Political Economy and Taxation* (London: John Murray, 1821), from the "Preface."
7. Edwin Cannan, "The Division of Income," *Quarterly Journal of Economics* 19, no. 3 (May 1905), pp. 341–69, at p. 363.
8. The marginal utility is the change in the total utility of a consumer from a change in her consumption basket.
9. The works mentioned are William Stanley Jevons, *The Theory of Political Economy* (London: Macmillan, 1871); Carl Menger, *Grundsätze der Volkswirtschaftslehre* [*Principles of Economics*] (Wien: Wilhelm Braumüller, 1871); Léon Walras, *Éléments d'économie politique pure*

[*Elements of Pure Economics: Or, the Theory of Social Wealth*] (Lausanne: Corbaz & Cie, 1874); and Alfred Marshall, *Principles of Economics* (London: Macmillan, 1890).

10. Dobb, *Theories of Value and Distribution since Adam Smith*, pp. 33–34.
11. The name comes from its authors, Charles Cobb and Paul Douglas. This contribution was originally presented by Paul H. Douglas in 1927 at the American Economic Association Conference and published the following year by Douglas and Charles W. Cobb as "A Theory of Production," *American Economic Review* 18 (March 1928), pp. 139–65; it was republished in Paul H. Douglas's *Theory of Wages* (London: Macmillan, 1934).
12. Dobb, *Theories of Value and Distribution since Adam Smith*, p. 172.
13. Hugh Dalton, preface to *Some Aspects of the Inequality of Incomes in Modern Communities* (London: Routledge, 1920, with a revised edition in 1925), p. vii. Pigou's slightly antecedent contributions are Alfred Cecil Pigou, *Wealth and Welfare* (New York: Macmillan, 1912), and *The Economics of Welfare* (London: Macmillan, 1920).
14. Dalton, *Some Aspects of the Inequality of Incomes in Modern Communities*, appendix to the 1925 edition, p. 2.
15. Lionel Robbins, *The Significance of Economic Science* (London: Allen & Unwin, 1932), chap. 6.
16. A longlasting discussion started from Robbins's position, shaped by Samuelson's 1947 stance on what economics should or should not take into consideration. See Anthony B. Atkinson, "Bringing Income Distribution in from the Cold," *Economic Journal* 107 (March 1997), pp. 297–321; idem, "The Strange Disappearance of Welfare Economics," *Kyklos* 54 (May–August 2001), pp. 193–206; idem, "Economics as a Moral Science," *Economica* 76 (April 2009), pp. 791–804; idem, "Economics as a Moral Science: The Restoration of Welfare Economics," *American Economic Review: Papers & Proceedings* 101, no. 3 (May 2011), pp. 157–61.
17. Dobb, *Theories of Value and Distribution since Adam Smith*, pp. 240–41 and 242.
18. Amartya K. Sen, *On Economic Inequality*, Radcliffe Lectures (Clarendon Press of Oxford University Press, 1972), p. 7.
19. Amartya K. Sen, "Ethical Measurement of Inequality: Some Difficulties," in *Personal Income Distribution*, edited by Willhelm Krelle and Anthony F. Shorrucks (Amsterdam: North-Holland, 1987), pp. 81–98. A quasi-coincident evaluation comes from Ezra Mishan at the end of

his monumental survey of welfare theories: "A study of welfare which confines itself to the measurement of quantities of goods and their distribution is not only seriously limited, it is ... positively misleading." See Ezra J. Mishan, "A Survey of Welfare Economics," *Economic Journal* 70, no. 278 (June 1960), pp. 197–265, at p. 256.

20. See Atkinson, "The Strange Disappearance of Welfare Economics"; idem, "Economics as a Moral Science"; idem, "Economics as a Moral Science: The Restoration of Welfare Economics."
21. Robert M. Solow, "Welfare and Work," in *The Tanner Lectures on Human Values,* vol. 19, edited by Nancy Fraser and Grethe B. Peterson (University of Utah Press, 1998), p. 213.
22. Milton Friedman, "Choice, Chance and the Personal Distribution of Income," *Journal of Political Economy* 61, no. 4 (August 1953), pp. 277–90, at pp. 277–78.
23. James E. Meade, *Efficiency, Equality and the Ownership of Property* (New York: Routledge, 1964).
24. Thomas Piketty, *Capital in the Twenty-First Century* (Belknap Press of Harvard University Press, 2014).
25. James E. Meade, "The Inheritance of Inequality," *The Keynes Lecture in Economics, Proceedings of the British Academy* 59 (London: March 1975), pp. 355–81, at p. 358.
26. Neal and Rosen provide the most recent survey of the main models of the distribution of earnings. See Derek Neal and Sherwin Rosen, "Theories of the Distribution of Earnings," in *Handbook of Income Distribution,* vol. 1, edited by Anthony B. Atkinson and François Bourguignon (Amsterdam: Elsevier, 2000), pp. 379–427.
27. John M. Keynes, *The General Theory of Employment, Interest and Money* (New York: Harcourt, Brace and Co., 1936), p. 374.
28. Nicholas Kaldor, "Alternative Theories of Distribution," *Review of Economic Studies* 23, no. 2 (1955–1956), pp. 83–100, at p. 94.
29. Robert S. Goldfarb and Thomas C. Leonard, "Inequality of What among Whom? Rival Conceptions of Distribution in the Twentieth Century," in *Research in the History of Economic Thought and Methodology,* vol. 23, pt. 1: *A Research Annual,* edited by Warren J. Samuels, Jeff E. Biddle, and Ross B. Emmett (Bingley, UK: Emerald Group Publishing, 2005), pp. 75–118.
30. Tibor Scitovsky, "A Survey of Some Theories of Income Distribution," in *The Behavior of Income Shares: Selected Theoretical and Empirical*

Issues: NBER Conference on Research in Income and Wealth, edited by Charles L. Schultze and Luis Weiner (Princeton University Press, 1964), pp. 15–51.

31. Melvin W. Reder, "A Partial Survey of the Theory of Income Size Distribution," in *Six Papers on the Size Distribution of Wealth and Income: Conference on the Size Distribution of Income and Wealth,* edited by Lee Soltow (University of Pennsylvania and NBER, 1969), pp. 205–50, at p. 205.
32. Atkinson, "Bringing Income Distribution in from the Cold," p. 299.
33. See Jan Tinbergen, "Substitution of Graduate by Other Labour," *Kyklos* 27, no. 2 (January 1974), pp. 217–26; idem, *Income Distribution: Analysis and Policies* (Amsterdam: North-Holland, 1975); and, more recently, Claudia Goldin and Lawrence F. Katz, *The Race between Education and Technology* (Harvard University Press, 2008).
34. Anthony B. Atkinson, "Income Inequality in OECD Countries: Data and Explanations," *CESifo Economic Studies* 49, no. 4 (2003), pp. 479–513. As an example of these few models, Atkinson quotes Herbert Simon, "The Compensation of Executives," *Sociometry* 20 (March 1957), pp. 32–35, and Harold F. Lydall, "The Distribution of Employment Income," *Econometrica* 27, no. 1 (January 1959), pp. 110–15, for the first aspect, and Sherwin Rosen, "The Economics of Superstars," *American Economic Review* 71, no. 5 (December 1981), pp. 845–58, and Robert H. Frank and Philip J. Cook, *The Winner-Take-All Society: Why the Few at the Top Get So Much More Than the Rest of Us* (New York: Free Press, 1995), for the second.
35. Atkinson, "Income Inequality in OECD Countries," p. 501.
36. Joseph A. Schumpeter, *History of Economic Analysis* (Oxford University Press, 1954), p. 645.
37. Friedman, "Choice, Chance, and the Personal Distribution of Income," p. 277; Atkinson, "Bringing Income Distribution in from the Cold," p. 298.
38. For a full discussion of this topic, see Agnar Sandmo, "The Principal Problem in Political Economy: Income Distribution in the History of Economic Thought," in *Handbook of Income Distribution,* vol. 2A, edited by Anthony B. Atkinson and François Bourguignon (London: Elsevier, 2014), pp. 3–66.

3. *The Statistical Drift of Inequality Studies*

1. Peter Lambert, "Editorial: Serge Kolm's The Optimal Production of Social Justice," *Journal of Economic Inequality* 5, no. 2 (February 2007), pp. 213–34, at p. 213.
2. "The collectivist State, more so than free competition, appears to be able to carry the equilibrium point onto the line of complete transformations ... To sum up, pure economics does not give us a truly decisive criterion for choosing between an organization of society based on private property and a socialist organization." Vilfredo Pareto, *Manual of Political Economy*, translated by Ann S. Schwier (New York: Augustus M. Kelley, 1971; English translation of the 1927 French translation of the original 1906 Italian version), chap. 6 and pp. 58–61.
3. Vilfredo Pareto, *Cours d'économie politique* (Losanna: Rouge, 1896–97; Genève: Librairie Droz, 1964), § 957.
4. "Il est absolument impossible d'admettre qu'il sont dus seulement au hazard." Pareto, *Cours*, § 960 (our translation).
5. "La nature même des hommes." Pareto, *Cours*, § 1012 (our translation).
6. Costantino Bresciani-Turroni, "Pareto's Law and the Index of Inequality of Incomes," *Econometrica* 7, no. 2 (April 1939), pp. 107–33.
7. For a complete technical presentation of these matters and contributions, see Christian Kleiber and Samuel Kotz, *Statistical Size Distributions in Economics and Actuarial Sciences* (Hoboken, NJ: Wiley & Sons, 2003).
8. Max Otto Lorenz, "Methods of Measuring the Concentration of Wealth," *Quarterly Publications of the American Statistical Association* 9, no. 70 (1905), pp. 209–19, at pp. 209, 213, and 217, respectively.
9. Willford I. King, *The Elements of Statistical Method* (New York: Macmillan, 1912), pp. 156–57.
10. Corrado Gini, *Sulla misura della concentrazione e della variabilità dei caratteri* (Venezia: Premiate officine grafiche C. Ferrari, 1913–14), § 6.
11. See the extensive portrait of Gini by Giovanni M. Giorgi, "Corrado Gini: The Man and the Scientist," *METRON* 69 (January 2011), pp. 1–28.
12. Corrado Gini, *Memorie di metodologia statistica*, vol. 1: *Variabilità e concentrazione* (Milano: Giuffrè, 1939).
13. Corrado Gini, "Sulla misura della concentrazione e della variabilità dei caratteri," in *Memorie di metodologia statistica*, vol. 1, pp. 361–408.

14. This is the "granularity," in technical terms.
15. The entropy is the informational content of any event, or sequence of events, and is supposed to decrease with the probability of realization of the event(s).
16. Robert Gibrat, *Les inégalités économiques; Aux inégalite's des richesses, à la concentration des entreprises, aux populations des villes, aux statistiques des familles, etc., d'une loi nouvelle, la loi de l'effet proportionnel* (Paris: Librairie du Recueil Sirey, 1931).
17. The central limit theorem is a fundamental theorem for many statistical procedures. For our purposes, it suffices to say that it relates to the convergence of a given distribution to a normal or a log-normal one, depending on certain assumptions about the random term.
18. Harold Lydall, *The Structure of Earnings* (Oxford University Press, 1968), p. 25.
19. This stream of research lasted almost fifty years. See, for example, the work of Henry L. Moore, *Laws of Wages: An Essay in Statistical Economics* (New York: Macmillan, 1911); Alfred C. Pigou, *The Economics of Welfare*, 4th ed. (London: Macmillan, 1932); Harold T. Davis, *The Theory of Econometrics* (Bloomington, Ind.: Principia Press, 1941); and Melvin W. Reder, "A Partial Survey of the Theory of Income Size Distribution," in *Six Papers on the Size Distribution of Wealth and Income*, edited by Lee Soltow (Columbia University and National Bureau of Economic Research, 1969), pp. 205–54.
20. The piecemeal literature on a theory of personal distribution includes Gurikbal S. Sahota, "Theories of Personal Income Distribution: A Survey," *Journal of Economic Literature* 16 (March 1978), pp. 1–55, a brilliant review of a huge constellation of theories, and Lydall, *The Structure of Earnings*, which reviews a more selective array of contributions. Another standard reference is Derek Neal and Sherwin Rosen, "Theories of the Distribution of Earnings," in *Handbook of Income Distribution*, vol. 1, edited by Anthony B. Atkinson and François Bourguignon (London: Elsevier, 2000), pp. 379–427.
21. David G. Champernowne, "A Model of Income Distribution," *Economic Journal* 63 (June 1953), pp. 318–51, at p. 319, and *The Distribution of Income between Persons* (Cambridge University Press, 1973), p. 190.
22. Jan Tinbergen, "On the Theory of Income Distribution," *Weltwirtschaftliches Archiv* 77 (1956), pp. 155–75, at p. 156.
23. Anthony B. Atkinson and François Bourguignon, "Introduction,"

in *Handbook of Income Distribution*, vol. 1, edited by Atkinson and Bourguignon, p. 5.

24. The monumental *Handbook of Income Distribution*, especially volume 2B, edited by Atkinson and Bourguignon in 2015 (complementing volume 1, published in 2000), provides a complete overview of the state of the art.
25. Simon Kuznets, "Economic Growth and Income Inequality," *American Economic Review* 45, no. 1 (March 1955), pp. 1–28.
26. Ibid., p. 4.
27. Ibid., p. 18.
28. Ibid., p. 23.
29. As noted in Bresciani-Turroni, "Pareto's Law and the Index of Inequality of Incomes," pp. 117–18.
30. Kuznets, "Economic Growth and Income Inequality," p. 26. As recalled by some scholars, "He also stressed that, even if the data turned out to be valid, they pertained to an extremely limited period of time and to exceptional historical experiences and that caution had therefore to be exercised in the conclusions drawn from his theory. Nevertheless, his caveats were jettisoned and his hypothesis raised to the level of law, becoming the basis for numerous formal models and elaborate econometric exercises, some of which lost touch with the complex reality that he was trying to uncover and characterize" (Robert W. Fogel and others, "The Scientific Methods of Simon Kuznets," in Robert W. Fogel and others, *Political Arithmetic: Simon Kuznets and the Empirical Tradition in Economics* [University of Chicago Press, 2013], pp. 89–105, at p. 103).
31. The transfer principle was first advanced by Arthur C. Pigou, *Wealth and Welfare* (London: Macmillan, 1912).
32. On the fundamental role of Dalton in inequality studies, see Andrea Brandolini, "Matematica e democrazia," in *Atti del convegno "Matematica e democrazia,"* Storia 39–40, edited by Angelo Guerraggio (Orvieto: PRISTEM, 2014), and Anthony B. Atkinson and Andrea Brandolini, "Unveiling the Ethics behind Inequality Measurement: Dalton's Contribution to Economics," *Economic Journal* 125 (March 2015), pp. 209–34.
33. Anthony B. Atkinson, "On the Measurement of Inequality," *Journal of Economic Theory* 2 (1970), pp. 244–63. See also Christian Kleiber, "The Lorenz Curve in Economics and Econometrics," in *Advances on Income Inequality and Concentration Measures: Collected Papers in Memory of*

Corrado Gini and Max O. Lorenz, edited by Gianni Betti and Achille Lemmi (London: Routledge, 2008), pp. 225–42.

34. Namely, symmetry, mean independence, the Pareto criterion, and the transfer principle. More than a decade later, Anthony Shorrocks extended Atkinson's finding, and additional results were reached also for the crossing case, for both situations in which individuals (or, more precisely, income units) have or do not have common needs. Anthony F. Shorrocks, "Ranking Income Distributions," *Economica* 50 (February 1983), pp. 3–17.
35. Technically, in Atkinson's words: "The index is equal to 1 minus the ratio of the equally distributed equivalent level of income to the mean of the actual distribution," where the former is "the level of income per head which if equally distributed would give the same level of social welfare as the present distribution" (Atkinson, "On the Measurement of Inequality," p. 250).
36. Ibid., p. 250
37. Peter J. Lambert recalls that Serge Kolm had already anticipated this idea in his "The Optimal Production of Social Justice," in which he coined the term *isophily* (liking equality) to characterize inequality aversion, a concept that would become a cornerstone of the subsequent analysis. See Peter J. Lambert, *The Distribution and Redistribution of Income*, 3rd ed. (Manchester University Press, 2001), and idem, "Editorial: Serge Kolm's The Optimal Production of Social Justice." Kolm's paper was presented at the Round Table Conference of the International Economic Association in Biarritz in 1965 and published in 1968 (French edition) and 1969 (English edition). It was partially republished in 2007 with the above editorial note by Peter Lambert. Atkinson acknowledges this fact, specifying: "I came to the subject from a different direction and only became aware of his work after my own article had been accepted for publication" (Atkinson and Brandolini, "Unveiling the Ethics behind Inequality Measurement," p. 212, note 4).
38. Amartya K. Sen, *On Economic Inequality*, expanded edition with a substantial annex by James E. Foster and Amartya K. Sen (Clarendon Press of Oxford University Press, 1997), p. 125. This judgment softens an earlier, more severe evaluation by Sen of Atkinson's paper: "It is still fairly restrictive to think of social welfare as a sum of individual welfare components," in *On Economic Inequality*, Radcliffe Lectures (Clarendon Press of Oxford University Press, 1972), p. 39.

39. Among Sen's numerous contributions, see "Equality of What?," in *The Tanner Lectures on Human Values,* vol. 1, edited by Sterling M. McMurrin (Cambridge University Press, 1980), pp. 197–220; *Commodities and Capabilities* (Amsterdam: North-Holland, 1985); and *Inequality Reexamined* (Harvard University Press, 1992).
40. "The Capability Approach," *Stanford Encyclopedia of Philosophy*, 2016 (http://plato.stanford.edu/entries/capability-approach/#FunCap).
41. See, for instance, David Aristei and Bruno Bracalente, "Measuring Multidimensional Inequality: Methods and Issues in Empirical Analysis," in *Statistical Methods and Applications from a Historical Perspective,* edited by Fabio Crescenzi and Stefania Mignani (Berlin: Springer, 2014), pp. 203–15, and Rolf Aaberge and Andrea Brandolini, "Multidimensional Poverty and Inequality," in *Handbook of Income Distribution,* vol. 2A, edited by Anthony B. Atkinson and François Bourguignon (Amsterdam: North-Holland, 2015), pp. 141–214.
42. More precisely, the subindicator for education is itself a composite index combining adult literacy with a two-thirds weight and gross enrollment in primary, secondary, and tertiary school with a one-third weight. All the components of the HDI are normalized by taking the proportional country's achievement over a pre-fixed scale.
43. This quotation comes from Anthony B. Atkinson, "Economics as a Moral Science," *Economica* 76 (2009), p. 802.

4. *Inequality and Globalization*

1. Christina Boswell, "Migration in Europe," paper prepared for the Policy Analysis and Research Programme of the Global Commission on International Migration (2005); Darrell Jackson and Alessia Passarelli, *Mapping Migration: Mapping Churches' Responses in Europe,* Churches' Commission for Migrants in Europe and Nova Research Centre (Nučice, Czech Republic: Gemma Press, 2008).
2. Susana Ferreira, "Migratory Crisis in the Mediterranean: Managing Irregular Flows," *Stability: International Journal of Security & Development* 5, no. 1 (2016), pp. 1–6, at p. 2; UNHCR, "Special Mediterranean Initiative: Plan for an Enhanced Operational Response. June–December 2015," June 16, 2015, update.
3. Mohammed Abdi, interviewed by *Le Monde* journalist Frédéric Bobin,

as reported in "Misurata, tra i migranti pronti alla traversata," *La Repubblica,* April 21, 2015, pp. 10–11.

4. United Nations and OECD, "World Migration in Figures," a joint contribution of UN-DESA and the OECD to the United Nations High-Level Dialogue on Migration and Development, October 3–4, 2013.
5. Jürgen Osterhammel and Niels P. Petersson, *Globalization: A Short History* (Princeton University Press, 2005). See also Jürgen Kocka, *Capitalism: A Short History* (Princeton University Press, 2016).
6. See, for example, Luigi Luca Cavalli-Sforza, *Genes, People, and Languages* (New York: North Point Press, 2000), and Jared Diamond, *Guns, Germs, and Steel: The Fates of Human Societies* (New York: W. W. Norton, 1997).
7. Osterhammel and Petersson, *Globalization,* p. 77.
8. For this reason, Osterhammel and Petersson have called globalization a "metaconcept" or a "macroprocess" (*Globalization,* p. 4).
9. Immanuel Wallerstein, *The Modern World-System,* vol. 1: *Capitalist Agriculture and the Origins of the European World-Economy in the Sixteenth Century* (San Diego, Calif.: Academic Press, 1974).
10. Fernand Braudel, *The Wheels of Commerce: Civilization & Capitalism, 15th–18th Century,* vol. 2 (New York: Harper & Row, 1982); idem, *The Perspective of the World: Civilization & Capitalism, 15th–18th Century,* vol. 3 (New York: Harper & Row, 1984); Giovanni Arrighi and Beverly J. Silver, *Chaos and Governance in the Modern World System* (University of Minnesota Press, 1999).
11. Karl Marx, *Capital: A Critique of Political Economy,* vol. 1, translated by Ben Fowkes, with an introduction by Ernest Mandel (New York: Vintage Books, 1977 [1867]), p. 915.
12. Jeffrey G. Williamson, *Globalization and the Poor Periphery before 1950* (MIT Press, 2006), p. 7.
13. François Bourguignon, *The Globalization of Inequality* (Princeton University Press, 2015), p. 5.
14. Branko Milanovic, *Worlds Apart: Measuring International and Global Inequality* (Princeton University Press, 2005), p. 31.
15. William J. Baumol, "Productivity Growth, Convergence, and Welfare: What the Long-Run Data Show," *American Economic Review* 76, no. 5 (1986), pp. 1072–85.
16. J. Bradford De Long, "Productivity Growth, Convergence, and Welfare: Comment," *American Economic Review* 78, no. 5 (1988), pp. 1138–54;

and William J. Baumol and Edward N. Wolff, "Productivity Growth, Convergence, and Welfare: Reply," *American Economic Review* 78, no. 5 (1988), pp. 1155–59.

17. Baumol, "Productivity Growth, Convergence, and Welfare," p. 1077 (emphasis in the original).
18. Lant Pritchett, "Divergence, Big Time," *Journal of Economic Perspectives* 11, no. 3 (1997), pp. 3–17, at p. 6.
19. De Long, "Productivity Growth, Convergence, and Welfare: Comment."
20. Lant Pritchett, "Divergence, Big Time."
21. Ibid.
22. Steve Dowrick and J. Bradford DeLong, "Globalization and Convergence," in *Globalization in Historical Perspective,* edited by Michael D. Bordo, Alan M. Taylor, and Jeffrey G. Williamson (University of Chicago Press, 2003), pp. 191–226.
23. Robert Barro, *Determinants of Economic Growth* (MIT Press, 1996).
24. Peter H. Lindert and Jeffrey G. Williamson, "Does Globalization Make the World More Unequal?," in *Globalization in Historical Perspective,* edited by Michael D. Bordo, Alan M. Taylor, and Jeffrey G. Williamson, pp. 227–71, at p. 230 (emphasis in the original).
25. Lindert and Williamson, "Does Globalization Make the World More Unequal?"
26. Ibid.
27. Ibid.
28. Angus Maddison, *The World Economy: A Millennial Perspective* (Paris: OECD, 2001), p. 22.
29. Lindert and Williamson, "Does Globalization Make the World More Unequal?," p. 255.
30. Ian M. D. Little, Tibor Scitovsky, and Maurice Scott, *Industry and Trade in Some Developing Countries: A Comparative Study* (Oxford University Press for the Development Centre of the Organization for Economic Cooperation and Development, 1970), pp. 14–15. For similarly influential analyses, see Bela Balassa and Associates, *The Structure of Protection in Developing Countries* (Johns Hopkins University Press, 1971); Jagdish Bhagwati, *Anatomy and Consequences of Exchange Control Regimes* (Cambridge, Mass.: Ballinger Publishing Co., 1978); and Anne O. Krueger, *Liberalization Attempts and Consequences* (Cambridge, Mass.: Ballinger Publishing Co., 1978).
31. Andrea Boltho and Gianni Toniolo, "The Assessment: The Twentieth

Century: Achievements, Failures, Lessons," *Oxford Review of Economic Policy* 15, no. 4 (1999), pp. 1–17.

32. Elaboration by Boltho and Toniolo from data by Angus Maddison and the World Bank. The Gini coefficients were obtained from population-weighted GDP per capita data at 1990 prices in PPP terms for forty-nine countries representing approximately 80 per cent of the world population. See Boltho and Toniolo, "The Assessment," esp. pp. 6–7.
33. World Bank, *World Development Report 1987: Barriers to Adjustment and Growth in the World Economy* (Oxford University Press for the World Bank, 1987); idem, *World Development Report 1994: Infrastructure for Development* (Oxford University Press for the World Bank, 1994).
34. World Bank, *Globalization, Growth, and Poverty: Building an Inclusive World Economy* (Oxford University Press and the World Bank, 2002), pp. 1–2.
35. Branko Milanovic, "The Two Faces of Globalization: Against Globalization as We Know It," *World Development* 31, no. 4 (2003), pp. 667–83, at pp. 667–68.
36. Ibid., p. 669 (emphasis in the original).
37. See, for example, the discussion in Paul Bairoch, *Economics and World History: Myths and Paradoxes* (University of Chicago Press, 1993), especially pt. 2, pp. 57–98; and Paul Bairoch, *Storia economica e sociale del mondo: Vittorie e insuccessi dal XVI secolo a oggi*, vol. 1 (Turin: Einaudi, 1999) (unfortunately, unavailable in English).
38. Milanovic, "The Two Faces of Globalization," p. 673.
39. This kind of analysis prompts two caveats: first, income comparisons among societies as different as the Roman Empire and eighteenth-century Holland imply many simplifications. Second, the very concept of income for societies whose population lived for the main part on production for self-consumption is difficult to apply and measure. A number of economists or economic historians focus on reconstructing data of this sort, which are, with all their limitations, a fundamental source for the work of economic historians and economists with an interest in history.
40. Branko Milanovic, Peter H. Lindert, and Jeffrey G. Williamson, "Pre-Industrial Inequality," *Economic Journal* 121, no. 551 (2011), pp. 255–72, esp. table 2, p. 263.
41. Ibid., p. 264.

42. Branko Milanovic, "Income Level and Income Inequality in the Euro-Mediterranean Region: From the Principate to the Islamic Conquest," January 2010, unpublished, figure 2, p. 16; idem, *Global Inequality, A New Approach for the Age of Globalization* (Belknap Press of Harvard University Press, 2016), pp. 50–51 and 66.
43. James K. Galbraith, *Inequality and Instability: A Study of the World Economy Just before the Great Crisis* (Oxford University Press, 2012), p. 48.
44. Thomas I. Palley, "The Accidental Controversialist: Deeper Reflections on Thomas Piketty's *Capital*," *Real-World Economics Review* 67 (May 2014), pp. 143–46. Palley refers to Giuseppe Tomasi di Lampedusa's 1958 novel *Il gattopardo* (*The Leopard* [Vintage, 2010]), in which the mid-nineteenth-century Principe di Salina confronts a deep change in Sicilian politics: the new generation of Sicilian nobility understands that, in the face of the social unrest that accompanied the political unification of Italy, old-style politics is useless to preserve the nobility's privileges. Paradoxically, the Sicilian aristocrats will be able to maintain their role and properties only if they lead the protests themselves. As the Principe's nephew argues, "If we want things to stay as they are, things will have to change" (p. 19). According to Palley, Piketty's analysis has the same function: "Piketty provides a mainstream neoclassical explanation of worsening inequality … that creates a gattopardo opportunity whereby inequality is folded back into mainstream economic theory which remains unchanged" ("The Accidental Controversialist," p. 144).
45. Thomas Piketty, *Capital in the Twenty-First Century* (Belknap Press of Harvard University Press, 2014). For a positive and highly informative review, see Branko Milanovic, "The Return of 'Patrimonial Capitalism': A Review of Thomas Piketty's *Capital in the Twenty-First Century*," *Journal of Economic Literature* 52, no. 2 (2014), pp. 519–34. Suzanne Helburn, "Rethinking Piketty: Critique of the Critiques (a Work in Progress)," *Real-World Economics Review* 75 (June 27, 2016), pp. 143–51, offers a comparative analysis of a number of reviews of Piketty's book. A harsh critique of Piketty's data visualization is in Noah Wright, "Data Visualization in *Capital in the 21st Century*," *World Social and Economic Review* 5 (2015), pp. 54–72. For collected analyses of Piketty's work, see *After Piketty: The Agenda for Economics and Inequality*, edited by Heather Boushey, J. Bradford DeLong, and Marshall Steinbaum

(Harvard University Press, 2017); *Piketty's Capital in the Twenty-First Century*, edited by Edward Fullbrook and Jamie Morgan (Bristol, UK: World Economics Association Books, 2017); and the monographic issues of the *British Journal of Sociology* 65, no. 4 (December 2014), and the *Review of Political Economy* 28, no. 2 (2016). For gattopardo economics as applied to Piketty's analysis, see, in addition to Palley's "The Accidental Controversialist," his "Gattopardo Economics: The Crisis and the Mainstream Response of Change That Keeps Things the Same," Institut für Makroökonomie und Konjunkturforschung, Working Paper 112 (April 2013). For mainstream criticisms of Piketty, see, for example, N. Gregory Mankiw, "Yes, $r > g$. So What?," *American Economic Review* 105, no. 5 (2015), pp. 43–47; and Daron Acemoglu and James A. Robinson, "The Rise and Decline of General Laws of Capitalism," *Journal of Economic Perspectives* 29, no. 1 (Winter 2015), pp. 3–28. For an assessment of this early wave of criticism, see J. Bradford DeLong, "The Melting Away of North Atlantic Social Democracy," TalkingPoints-Memo.com (http://talkingpointsmemo.com/features/marchtoinequality/fourmeltingsocialdemocracy/).

46. Anthony Brewer, *Marxist Theories of Imperialism: A Critical Survey*, 2nd ed. (London: Routledge, 1990). For a synthesis of this line of inquiry and how it can be imported into current discussions about wars and inequality trends, see Milanovic, *Global Inequality*, pp. 93–97.
47. Francis Fukuyama, "The End of History?," *National Interest* 16 (Summer 1989), pp. 3–18, at pp. 3–4. The article was later expanded into a book: Francis Fukuyama, *The End of History and the Last Man* (New York: Free Press, 1992).
48. François Bourguignon and Christian Morrisson, "Inequality among World Citizens: 1820–1992," *American Economic Review* 92, no. 4 (2002), pp. 727–44, at p. 727.
49. Milanovic, *Global Inequality*, p. 119.
50. Bourguignon and Morrisson, "Inequality among World Citizens," p. 728.
51. Milanovic, *Global Inequality*, p. 121.
52. Branko Milanovic, "True World Income Distribution, 1988 and 1993: First Calculation Based on Household Surveys Alone," *Economic Journal* 112, no. 476 (2002), pp. 51–92, at p. 55.
53. Branko Milanovic, "Global Inequality of Opportunity: How Much of Our Income Is Determined by Where We Live?," *Review of Economics and Statistics* (May 2015), p. 97, note 2, and pp. 452–60.

54. For an interesting analysis of the unintended consequences of the extension of the US wall on the border with Mexico, see Adam Tooze, "Donald Trump's Wall Is No Bar to Migration from Mexico: The People of Border Regions Have Always Been Entangled," *Financial Times*, February 6, 2017.
55. Milanovic, *Global Inequality*. For a discussion of the reclined S, see Branko Milanovic, *The Haves and the Have-Nots: A Brief and Idiosyncratic History of Global Inequality* (New York: Basic Books, 2011), pp. 83–91.
56. Galbraith, *Inequality and Instability*, pp. 47–53.
57. Milanovic, *Global Inequality*, p. 122. Other data from the World Bank, however, show a decline starting as early as the 1980s and increasing in velocity after the 1990s, and especially after the 2000s. See figure 4.1 in Milanovic, *Global Inequality*, p. 166. As we are dealing with a relatively short period and researchers have difficulty estimating accurately the highest incomes, Milanovic argues that "the most accurate statement would be that the evidence suggests that global income inequality is either stable or on a decline" (*Global Inequality*, p. 123).
58. Milanovic, *Global Inequality*, p. 166.
59. Ibid., pp. 10–11 and 18–24.

5. *Inequality and Democracy: An Open Issue*

1. Ariana Strandburg-Peshkin, Damien Farine, Iain D. Couzin, and Margaret C. Crofoot, "Shared Decision-making Drives Collective Movement in Wild Baboons," *Science* 348, no. 6241 (June 19, 2015).
2. The possible effects of democracy on inequality – the degree to which the distribution of political rights influences economic distribution – go beyond this book. They emerge tangentially, however, in the discussion of the lock-in (when not self-reinforcing) effects on inequality that cooccur with a shrinking of the democratic space. On this issue, see Mark Gradstein and Branko Milanovic, "Does Liberté = Egalité? A Survey of the Empirical Links between Democracy and Inequality with Some Evidence on the Transition Economies," World Bank Policy Research Working Paper 2875, August 2002.
3. "In its inception democracy was a project simply blind to economic inequality, regardless of how revolutionary it may have been politically.

Morally based arguments for redistribution ... were marginal or ephemeral" (Adam Przeworski, *Democracy and the Limits of Self-Government* [Cambridge University Press, 2010], p. 85). On the same position, see Nadia Urbinati, *Democracy Disfigured* (Harvard University Press, 2014), chap. 1.

4. Robert Alan Dahl, *On Democracy* (Yale University Press, 1998), has beautiful passages on why we should adopt the principle of political equality.
5. See Luciano Canfora, *Democracy in Europe: A History of an Ideology* (London: Wiley, 2005), and John Dunn, *Setting the People Free: The Story of Democracy* (London: Atlantic Books, 2015).
6. See Philippe Schmitter and Terry Lynn Karl, "What Democracy Is ... and Is Not," *Journal of Democracy* 2 (Summer 1991), pp. 75–88.
7. Dahl, *On Democracy* (2000 edition), p. 38.
8. Ibid., p. 42.
9. Larry Diamond, *The Spirit of Democracy* (London: Holt, 2008), p. 21.
10. Larry Diamond and Leonardo Morlino, "The Quality of Democracy: An Overview," *Journal of Democracy* 15, no. 4 (October 2004), pp. 20–31, at p. 21.
11. Edward L. Glaeser, "Inequality," in *The Oxford Handbook of Political Economy*, edited by Donald Wittman and Barry Weingast (Oxford University Press, 2006), pp. 624–41.
12. Daron Acemoglu, Simon Johnson, and James A. Robinson, "Institutions as the Fundamental Cause of Long-Run Growth," in *Handbook of Economic Growth*, vol. 1A, edited by Philippe Aghion and Steven N. Durlauf (Amsterdam: Elsevier/North-Holland, 2005), pp. 385–472.
13. A complex analysis is hidden behind the simple statement that *the governments make and implement policies that the citizens want.* For instance, some policies need qualified expertise, and citizens may not be able to evaluate them; politicians and governments may be manipulative in order to fulfill their goals and interests; international commitments may constrain the political choices, and so on.
14. Jeffrey A. Winters, *Oligarchy* (Cambridge University Press, 2011), p. 208.
15. Guillermo A. O'Donnell, "Do Economists Know Best?," *Journal of Democracy* 6, no. 1 (January 1995), pp. 23–28, at p. 27, and Guillermo O'Donnell, quoted in Terry Lynn Karl, "Economic Inequality and Democratic Instability," *Journal of Democracy* 11, no. 1 (January 2000), pp. 149–56, at p. 150, respectively.

16. Adam Przeworski, "Self-enforcing Democracy," in *The Oxford Handbook of Political Economy*, edited by Wittman and Weingast, pp. 312–28, at p. 312.
17. This evergreen theorem was originally introduced in Duncan Black, "On the Rationale of Group Decision-making," *Journal of Political Economy* 56, no. 1 (February 1948), pp. 23–34, and later developed in Kevin W. S. Roberts, "Voting over Income Tax Schedule," *Journal of Public Economics* 8, no. 3 (1977), pp. 329–40, and Allan H. Meltzer and Scott F. Richard, "A Rational Theory of the Size of Government," *Journal of Political Economy* 89 (October 1981), pp. 914–27.
18. See Gene M. Grossman and Elhanan Helpman, *Special Interest Politics* (MIT Press, 2001).
19. Branko Milanovic, "The Median-Voter Hypothesis, Income Inequality, and Income Redistribution: An Empirical Test with the Required Data," *European Journal of Political Economy* 16 (2000), pp. 367–410; Larry M. Bartels, *Unequal Democracy: The Political Economy of the New Gilded Age* (Princeton University Press, 2008), p. 27.
20. See Bartels, *Unequal Democracy*, and Przeworski, *Democracy and the Limits of Self-Government.*
21. "Senators attached no weight at all to the views of constituents in the bottom third of the income distribution – the constituents whose economic interests were obviously most directly at stake ... The views of middle-income constituents seem to have been only slightly more influential ... Senators' voting decisions were largely driven by the ideological predilections of their affluent constituents" (Bartels, *Unequal Democracy*, p. 265). Bartels himself reports the other studies – always on the United States – whose results go in the same direction as his.
22. Paul Krugman, *The Conscience of a Liberal* (New York: W. W. Norton, 2007); Jacob S. J. Hacker and Paul Pierson, *The Winner-Take-All Politics* (New York: Simon & Schuster, 2010). For the tilt of responsiveness toward affluent citizens, see Martin Gilens, *Affluence and Influence: Economic Inequality and Political Power in America* (Princeton University Press, 2012), p. 1.
23. Richard Wilkinson and Kate Pickett, *The Spirit Level: Why Greater Equality Makes Societies Stronger* (London: Allen Lane, 2009). Notwithstanding its great appeal, the book has been criticized for cherry-picking observations and for some confusion between correlation and causal-

ity. For a substantive critique, see, for instance, David Runciman, "How Messy It All Is," *London Review of Books* 31, no. 20 (October 22, 2009), pp. 3–6.

24. Brian Nolan and others, *Changing Inequalities and Societal Impacts in Rich Countries: Thirty Countries' Experience* (Oxford University Press, 2014); Wiemer Salverda and others, *Changing Inequalities in Rich Countries: Analytical and Comparative Perspectives* (Oxford University Press, 2014).
25. See Angus Deaton, *The Great Escape: Health, Wealth, and the Origins of Inequality* (Princeton University Press, 2013), p. 7.
26. Alan B. Krueger, "The Rise and Consequences of Inequality in the United States," speech given at the Center for American Progress on January 12, 2012, based on data and earlier work by Miles Corak, "Inequality from Generation to Generation: The United States in Comparison," in *The Economics of Inequality, Poverty, and Discrimination in the 21st Century*, edited by Robert S. Rycroft (Santa Barbara: ABC-CLIO, 2013), pp. 107–26. For low mobility in the United States, see Markus Jäntti and others, "American Exceptionalism in a New Light: A Comparison of Intergenerational Earnings Mobility in the Nordic Countries, the United Kingdom and the United States," Discussion Paper 1938 (Bonn: Institute for the Study of Labor IZA, January 2006). As Miles Corak notes, "In the United States, about 50% of educational and wealth disadvantage is passed on by the parents." See Corak, "Do Poor Children Become Poor Adults? Lessons from a Cross Country Comparison of Generational Earnings Mobility," Discussion Paper 1993 (Bonn: Institute for the Study of Labor IZA, March 2006).
27. Corak, "Inequality from Generation to Generation," p. 108.
28. Larry M. Bartels, "Economic Inequality and Political Representation," in *The Unsustainable American State,* edited by Lawrence Jacobs and Desmond King (Oxford University Press, 2009), pp. 167–96, at p. 167.
29. See, among others, Bartels, *Unequal Democracy,* and Przeworski, *Democracy and the Limits of Self-Government.*
30. André Blais and Daniel Rubenson, "The Source of Turnout Decline: New Values or New Contexts?," *Comparative Political Studies* 46, no. 1 (January 2013), pp. 95–117.
31. Willem H. Buiter, "Economists Forum," *Financial Times,* February 14, 2007.

32. Milton Friedman, "Choice, Chance and the Personal Distribution of Income," *Journal of Political Economy* 61, no. 4 (August 1953), pp. 277–90, at pp. 277.
33. Giuseppe Bertola, "Factor Shares and Savings in Endogenous Growth," *American Economic Review* 83, no. 5 (February 1993), pp. 1184–98; Alberto Alesina and Dani Rodrik, "Distributive Politics and Economic Growth," *Quarterly Journal of Economics* 109 (May 1994), pp. 465–90; Torsten Persson and Guido Tabellini, "Is Inequality Harmful for Growth?," *American Economic Review* 84, no. 3 (June 1994), pp. 600–21; Roberto Perotti, "Growth, Income Distribution and Democracy: What the Data Say," *Journal of Economic Growth* 1 (June 1996), pp. 149–87; Alberto Alesina and Roberto Perotti, "Income Distribution, Political Instability, and Investment," *European Economic Review* 40, no. 6 (1996), pp. 1203–28; Roland Benabou, "Unequal Societies," NBER Working Paper 5583 (Cambridge, Mass., May 1996); Jonathan D. Ostry, Andrew Berg, and Charalambos G.Tsangarides, "Redistribution, Inequality and Growth," International Monetary Fund Staff Discussion Note, February 2014; and Federico Cingano, "Trends in Income Inequality and Its Impact on Economic Growth," Working Paper 163 (Paris: OECD Social, Employment and Migration, 2014).
34. See, for example, Cingano, "Trends in Income Inequality"; Ostry and others, "Redistribution, Inequality and Growth"; and Bertola, "Factor Shares and Savings in Endogenous Growth."
35. See Alesina and Perotti, "Income Distribution, Political Instability, and Investment"; and Dani Rodrik, "Where Did All the Growth Go? External Shocks, Social Conflict, and Growth Collapses," *Journal of Economic Growth* 4 (December 1999), pp. 385–412.
36. See, for example, Matthew A. Baum and David A. Lake, "The Political Economy of Growth: Democracy and Human Capital," *American Journal of Political Science* 47, no. 2 (2003), pp. 333–47; Glaeser, "Inequality"; Matteo Cervellati, Piergiuseppe Fortunato, and Uwe Sunde, "Are All Democracies Equally Good? The Role of Interactions between Political Environment and Inequality for Rule of Law," Discussion Paper 2984 (Bonn: Institute for the Study of Labor IZA, August 2007); and Florian Jung and Uwe Sunde, "Inequality, Development and the Stability of Democracy: Lipset and Three Critical Junctures in German History," Discussion Paper DP8406 (London: Centre for Economic Policy Research, June 2011).

37. Joseph E. Stiglitz, *The Great Divide* (New York: W. W. Norton, 2015), p. 223.
38. Kristin J. Forbes, "A Reassessment of the Relationship Between Inequality and Growth," *American Economic Review* 90 (September 2000), pp. 869–87; Abhijit V. Banerjee and Esther Duflo, "Inequality and Growth: What Can the Data Say?," *Journal of Economic Growth* 8 (June 2003), pp. 267–99.
39. Salvatore Morelli, "Rising Inequality and Macroeconomic Stability," in *After Piketty: The Agenda for Economics and Inequality*, edited by Heather Boushey, J. Bradford DeLong, and Marshall Steinbaum (Harvard University Press, 2017), pp. 412–35, at p. 435.
40. Dani Rodrik, "Good and Bad Inequality," *Project Syndicate*, December 11, 2014.
41. Adam Przeworski and Michael Wallerstein, "Structural Dependence of the State on Capital," *American Political Science Review* 82, no. 1 (March 1988), pp. 11–29.
42. Adam Przeworski, "Democracy, Equality, and Redistribution," in *Political Judgment: Essays in Honor of John Dunn*, edited by Richard Bourke and Raymond Geuss (Cambridge University Press, 2009), p. 26.
43. Stewart Lansley, *The Cost of Inequality* (London: Gibson Square, 2012), p. 103.
44. Robert Reich, *Supercapitalism* (London: Icon books, 2008); Andrew Glyn, *Capitalism Unleashed* (Oxford University Press, 2006); Joseph E. Stiglitz, "US Does Not Have Capitalism Now," CNBC, January 19, 2010; Edward N. Luttwak, *Turbo-Capitalism: Winners & Losers in the Global Economy* (New York: HarperCollins, 1999). The last quotation is from Stiglitz, *The Great Divide*, p. 126.
45. "Postdemocracy" is a term coined in 2000 by the British political scientist Colin Crouch to describe a location on the downward-sloping part of the democracy parabola: the democratic system is fully operational, but its application is increasingly restricted. See Crouch, *Coping with Post-Democracy* (London: Fabian Society, 2000).
46. Claus Offe, "Democracy in Crisis: Two and a Half Theories about the Operation of Democratic Capitalism," *Open Democracy*, July 9, 2012.

6. *The Future of Inequality*

1. Richard H. Tawney, *Equality* (New York: Harcourt, Brace and Co., 1931), p. 50.
2. William E. Gladstone, quoted in Matthew Arnold, "Equality," address delivered at the Royal Institution, *Fortnightly Review* 135, New Series 23 (March 1, 1878), pp. 313–34, at pp. 314–15.
3. Thomas Piketty, *Capital in the Twenty-First Century* (Belknap Press of Harvard University Press, 2014).
4. For references pertaining to criticism of Piketty's work, see note 45 in chapter 4.
5. IRS, Statistical Data Section, "Personal Exemptions and Individual Income Tax Rates, 1913–2002" (www.irs.gov/pub/irs-soi/02inpetr.pdf); IRS, "Federal Tax Rates, Personal Exemptions, and Standard Deductions," various years; Federal Reserve Bank of Minneapolis, "Consumer Price Index (Estimate) 1800–."
6. James Tobin, "Prospects for Macro-Economic Policy," in *The New Economics One Decade Older* (Princeton University Press, 1974), esp. pp. 88–93; idem, "A Proposal for International Monetary Reform," *Eastern Economic Journal* 4, nos. 3/4 (July–October 1978), pp. 153–59.
7. For a concise but comprehensive discussion of these themes, see Joseph E. Stiglitz, *The Price of Inequality: How Today's Divided Society Endangers Our Future* (New York: W. W. Norton, 2013), pp. 336–63; and James K. Galbraith, *Inequality: What Everyone Needs to Know* (Oxford University Press, 2016), pp. 135–49.
8. Anthony Atkinson, "Inequality: What Can Be Done about It?," *Social Europe*, September 14, 2016. See also idem, *Inequality: What Can Be Done?* (Harvard University Press, 2015).
9. Ibid.
10. Jan Tinbergen, "Substitution of Graduate by Other Labour," *Kyklos* 27, no. 2 (1974), pp. 217–26; Claudia Goldin and Lawrence F. Katz, *The Race between Education and Technology* (Belknap Press of Harvard University Press, 2010).
11. Goldin and Katz, *The Race between Education and Technology.*
12. David Card and John E. DiNardo, "Skill-Biased Technological Change and Rising Wage Inequality: Some Problems and Puzzles," *Journal of Labor Economics* 20, no. 4 (2002), pp. 733–83; James K. Galbraith, *Cre-*

ated Unequal: The Crisis in American Pay (New York: Free Press, 1998); James K. Galbraith, *Inequality and Instability: A Study of the World Economy Just before the Great Crisis* (Oxford University Press, 2012). See also Anthony B. Atkinson, "The Changing Distribution of Income: Evidence and Explanations," *German Economic Review* 1, no. 1 (2000), pp. 3–18.

13. Jeff Madrick, *Seven Bad Ideas: How Mainstream Economists Have Damaged America and the World* (New York: Alfred A. Knopf, 2014).
14. Heather Beth Johnson, *The American Dream and the Power of Wealth: Choosing School and Inheriting Inequality in the Land of Opportunity* (New York: Routledge, 2015), pp. 13–14.
15. Samuel Bowles, Steven N. Durlauf, and Karla Hoff, eds., *Poverty Traps* (Princeton University Press, 2016). On the vicious circles created by inequality, see also chapter 5.
16. *Income Inequality in the United States: Hearing Before the Joint Economic Committee,* 113th Cong. (2014), 2d Sess., S. Hrg. 113-202 (statement of Melissa Kearney), January 16.
17. Ibid.
18. Miles Corak, "Income Inequality, Equality of Opportunity, and Intergenerational Mobility," *Journal of Economic Perspectives* 27, no. 3 (July 2013), pp. 79–102.
19. President Barack Obama, "Remarks by the President on Economic Mobility," Town Hall Education Arts Recreation Campus, Washington, December 4, 2013.
20. Joseph E. Stiglitz, *Globalization and Its Discontents* (New York: W. W. Norton, 2002), p. 18, emphasis in the original; see also, in the same volume, pp. 180–94. Stiglitz's proposals on how to pace reforms in the global economy are more comprehensively discussed in his subsequent work, *Making Globalization Work* (New York: W. W. Norton, 2006). See also Dani Rodrik, *One Economics, Many Recipes: Globalization, Institutions, and Economic Growth* (Princeton University Press, 2009).
21. See Douglass C. North, John Joseph Wallis, and Barry R. Weingast, *Violence and Social Order: A Conceptual Framework for Interpreting Recorded Human History* (Cambridge University Press, 2009), and Daron Acemoglu and James A. Robinson, *Why Nations Fail: The Origins of Power, Prosperity, and Poverty* (New York: Crown, 2012).

22. For an introduction to the functioning and role of the gatekeeping state in Africa's history, see Frederick Cooper, *Africa since 1940: The Past of the Present* (Cambridge University Press, 2002).
23. Madrick, *Seven Bad Ideas*, p. 82. See also Ha-Joon Chang, *Kicking Away the Ladder: Development Strategy in Historical Perspective* (London: Anthem Press, 2003).
24. For an excellent example of the search for highly contextualized economic analysis, see *In Search of Prosperity: Analytical Narratives on Economic Growth*, edited by Dani Rodrik (Princeton University Press, 2003). For the World Bank's admission of the inadequacy of a one-size-fits-all approach, see World Bank, *Economic Growth in the 1990s: Learning from a Decade of Reform* (Washington: World Bank, 2005). For World Bank–sponsored research on an institutional framework for development, see Douglass C. North, John Joseph Wallis, Steven B. Webb, and Barry R. Weingast, "Limited Access Orders in the Developing World: A New Approach to the Problem of Development," World Bank Policy Research Working Paper 4359 (Washington: World Bank, 2007); and Douglass North, John Wallis, and Barry Weingast, "Violence and Social Orders," in Douglass North, Daron Acemoglu, Francis Fukuyama, and Dani Rodrik, *Governance, Growth, and Development Decision-making* (Washington: World Bank, 2008), pp. 9–16. More in general, development economics has increasingly become an applied branch of economics, thus shifting its focus from grand theories to analyses and models that apply to specific situations, see Michele Alacevich, "Theory and Practice in Development Economics," *History of Political Economy* 49, no. 5 (2017), pp. 264–91. For a criticism of the methodological approach of asking smaller questions about "what works" in development economics, and especially of its fashionable version of randomized controlled trials, see Sanjay Reddy, "Randomise This! On Poor Economics," *Review of Agrarian Studies* 2, no. 2 (July–December 2012), pp. 60–73.
25. Branko Milanovic, *Global Inequality: A New Approach for the Age of Globalization* (Belknap Press of Harvard University Press, 2016), p. 232. Degrowth theories, inspired by the seminal work of Nicholas Georgescu-Roegen, take a different stance. See his *The Entropy Law and the Economic Process* (Harvard University Press, 1971).
26. See the discussion in François Bourguignon, *The Globalization of Inequality* (Princeton University Press, 2016), pp. 117–45.

27. A thought-provoking analysis is Paul Collier, *Exodus: How Migration Is Changing Our World* (Oxford University Press, 2013).
28. Joseph E. Stiglitz, *The Euro, and Its Threat to the Future of Europe* (London: Allen Lane, 2016), p. 343.
29. Milanovic, *Global Inequality*, p. 230.
30. Data from Bourguignon, *The Globalization of Inequality*, p. 148, and Collier, *Exodus*, p. 207. According to Collier, official development aid is even less than the amount proposed by Bourguignon, and thus remittances are proportionally four times as much as development aid.
31. Jeffrey D. Sachs, *The End of Poverty: Economic Possibilities for Our Time* (New York: Penguin, 2006).
32. Camelia Minoiu and Sanjay G. Reddy, "Development Aid and Economic Growth: A Positive Long-Run Relation," *Quarterly Review of Economics and Finance* 50, no. 1 (February 2010), pp. 27–39.
33. Angus Deaton, *The Great Escape: Health, Wealth, and the Origins of Inequality* (Princeton University Press, 2013), p. 282.
34. Ibid., pp. 312–24. William Easterly, *The Elusive Quest for Growth: Economists' Adventures and Misadventures in the Tropics* (MIT Press, 2001); idem, *The White Man's Burden: Why the West's Efforts to Aid the Rest Have Done So Much Ill and So Little Good* (London: Penguin, 2006); idem, *The Tyranny of Experts: Economists, Dictators, and the Forgotten Rights of the Poor* (New York: Basic Books, 2014).

Appendix

1. It goes without saying that many important works offer information on these concepts. In addition to the more recent works that we have cited in this book, Anthony Atkinson's *The Economics of Inequality* (Oxford: Clarendon Press, 1975) remains an invaluable reference.
2. Joseph E. Stiglitz, Amartya Sen, and Jean-Paul Fitoussi, *Report by the Commission on the Measurement of Economic Performance and Social Progress* (available at www.stiglitz-sen-fitoussi.fr, 2009–2010).
3. More precisely, as recalled in chapter 3, it is a simple average of per capita income, life expectancy and educational achievement, which in turn is a compounded average of the adult population education and of the young population schooling.
4. Wealth also affects inequality, but income remains the main focus of

inequality studies because of the greater difficulty of collecting data on wealth, which are often incomplete and unreliable. As a consequence of these data limitations, economic inequality is commonly conceived as income inequality, though one should be aware that income inequality is conceptually narrower than economic inequality.

5. Angus Deaton and Salman Zaidi, "Guidelines for Constructing Consumption Aggregates for Welfare Analysis," Living Standards Measurement Study Working Paper Series 135 (Washington: World Bank, 2002), p. 1.
6. These three calculations of GDP, based respectively on production, expenditures, and incomes, can be considered nearly equivalent, though in an open economy net income from abroad must also be considered. Empirical studies on less developed countries often focus on consumption data, which are more easily available and more reliable than production data, because of the important role the shadow economy typically plays in these countries. At the same time, by definition consumption data do not capture savings. Hence, expenditure data tend to show lower inequality than income data.
7. Data from World Bank, GDP Per Capita (Constant 2010 US$). (http://data.worldbank.org/indicator/NY.GDP.PCAP.KD).
8. Data from World Bank, GDP at Market Prices (Constant 2010 US$). (http://data.worldbank.org/indicator/NY.GDP.MKTP.KD), and World Bank, Population, Total (http://data.worldbank.org/indicator/SP.POP.TOTL).
9. The World Bank reports the following population figures for 2015: China's population of 1,371,220,000; world population of 7,346,633,040.
10. Data from World Bank, GDP Per Capita (Constant 2010 US$). (http://data.worldbank.org/indicator/NY.GDP.PCAP.KD).
11. François Bourguignon, *The Globalization of Inequality* (Princeton University Press, 2015); Branko Milanovic, *Worlds Apart: Measuring International and Global Inequality* (Princeton University Press, 2005).
12. For a brief discussion of the three concepts of inequality, see Milanovic, *Worlds Apart*, pp. 7–11.
13. For an accessible discussion of the pros and cons of household surveys, see Branko Milanovic, *Global Inequality: A New Approach for the Age of Globalization* (Belknap Press of Harvard University Press, 2016), pp. 12–13.

14. For a detailed discussion of how the ICP works, see World Bank. *Measuring the Real Size of the World Economy: The Framework, Methodology, and Results of the International Comparison Program – ICP* (Washington: World Bank, 2013).
15. World Bank, International Comparison Project, History (http://go.worldbank.org/WLPETUYSO0).
16. Milanovic, *Global Inequality*, p. 15.
17. Ibid., pp. 16–17.
18. For the official market exchange rates, see World Bank, Official Exchange Rate (LCU Per US$, Period Average) (http://data.worldbank.org/indicator/PA.NUS.FCRF). For the PPP conversion factor, see World Bank, Price Level Ratio of PPP Conversion Factor (GDP) to Market Exchange Rate (http://data.worldbank.org/indicator/PA.NUS.PPPC.RF).
19. For more in-depth analyses, see *Handbook of Income Distribution*, edited by Anthony Atkinson and François Bourguignon (Amsterdam: Elsevier/North-Holland, 2000), and *The Economics of Poverty and Inequality*, edited by Frank A. Cowell (Cheltenham, UK: Edward Elgar, 2003).
20. Joseph Stiglitz, "Of the 1%, by the 1%, for the 1%," *Vanity Fair*, March 31, 2011.
21. Bourguignon, *The Globalization of Inequality*, p. 18.
22. José Gabriel Palma, "Homogeneous Middles vs. Heterogeneous Tails, and the End of the 'Inverted-U': The Share of the Rich Is What It's All About," Cambridge Working Papers in Economics 1111 (University of Cambridge, January 2011), p. 17, emphasis in the original.
23. See, for example, Ha-Joon Chang, *Economics: The User's Guide: A Pelican Introduction* (London: Penguin, 2014), pp. 328–29.
24. James K. Galbraith, *Inequality: What Everyone Needs to Know* (Oxford University Press, 2016), p. 62.
25. Branko Milanovic, All the Ginis (ALG) data set (version: October 2016). This data set imports data from nine different data sets to create a single standardized Gini indicator. All values are based on nationally representative household surveys that are comparable at the microlevel. For a description of how this data set is constructed, see Branko Milanovic, "Description of *All the Ginis* Dataset," October 2016, mimeo, available on Branko Milanovic's webpage on the website of the Stone Center on Socio-Economic Inequality, CUNY Graduate Center, New York. For an

assessment of this and other data sets, confirming the reliability of the ALG data set, see Timothy Smeeding and Jonathan P. Latner, "Povcal-Net, WDI and 'All the Ginis': A Critical Review," *Journal of Economic Inequality* 13, no. 4 (December 2015), pp. 603–28.

26. This is true for sufficiently large populations. The shape of the Lorenz curve with very small populations is different.
27. Galbraith, *Inequality and Instability*, p. 11.
28. Ibid., p. 12.
29. As Galbraith puts it, "Our measure of disparity of pay across industrial sectors is a very good ... approximation of survey-based measures of income or expenditure inequality" (ibid., p. 15).
30. Klaus Deininger and Lyn Squire, "A New Data Set Measuring Income Inequality," *World Bank Economic Review* 10, no. 3 (September 1996), pp. 565–91.
31. The WDI is based on household survey microdata, which is a major improvement with respect to the original Deiniger-Squire data set. Researchers, however, cannot access the microdata, only the harmonized metadata.
32. For a discussion of the Deininger-Squire data set with particular regard to OECD countries, see Anthony Atkinson and Andrea Brandolini, "Promise and Pitfalls in the Use of 'Secondary' Data-Sets: Income Inequality in OECD Countries as a Case Study," *Journal of Economic Literature* 39, no. 3 (September 2001), pp. 771–99.
33. Leonardo Gasparini and Leopoldo Tornarolli, "A Review of the OECD Income Distribution Database," *Journal of Economic Inequality* 13, no. 4 (December 2015), pp. 579–602.
34. For the LIS report on ten OECD countries, see Anthony B. Atkinson, Lee Rainwater, and Timothy M. Smeeding, "Income distribution in the OECD countries," *OECD Social Policy Studies*, no. 18 (Paris: OECD, 1995). See also Smeeding and Latner, "PovcalNet, WDI and 'All the Ginis.'" For a critical assessment of LIS, see Martin Ravallion, "The Luxembourg Income Study," *Journal of Economic Inequality* 13, no. 4 (December 2015), pp. 527–47, and Janet C. Gornick, Markus Jäntti, Teresa Munzi, and Thierry Kruten, "Luxembourg Income Study: Response," *Journal of Economic Inequality* 13, no. 4 (December 2015), pp. 549–56.
35. Smeeding and Latner, "PovcalNet, WDI and 'All the Ginis.'"
36. Frederick Solt, "The Standardized World Income Inequality Database,"

Social Science Quarterly 97, no. 5 (November 2016), pp. 1267–81, at p. 1279.

37. Galbraith, *Inequality and Instability*, pp. 32–33.
38. Emmanuel Saez, "The Research Agenda after *Capital in the Twenty-First Century*," in *After Piketty: The Agenda for Economics and Inequality*, edited by Heather Boushey, J. Bradford DeLong, and Marshall Steinbaum (Harvard University Press, 2017), pp. 304–21, at p. 306.
39. Anthony B. Atkinson and Andrea Brandolini, "On Data: A Case Study of the Evolution of Income Inequality across Time and across Countries," *Cambridge Journal of Economics* 33, no. 3 (May 2009), pp. 381–404, at p. 400.

Index